how2become

IELTS General Training & Academic Study Practice Guide

(Includes 270+ Questions)

www.How2Become.com

Orders: Please contact www.How2Become.com

You can order through Amazon.co.uk under ISBN 9781912370382, via the website www.How2Become.com, Gardners or Bertrams.

ISBN: 9781912370382

First published in 2018 by How2Become Ltd.

Typeset for How2Become Ltd by Gemma Butler.

Printed and bound by CPI Group (UK) Ltd, Croydon, CR0 4YY

Disclaimer

Every effort has been made to ensure that the information contained within this guide is accurate at the time of publication. How2Become Ltd is not responsible for anyone failing any part of any selection process as a result of the information contained within this guide. How2Become Ltd and their authors cannot accept any responsibility for any errors or omissions within this guide, however caused. No responsibility for loss or damage occasioned by any person acting, or refraining from action, as a result of the material in this publication can be accepted by How2Become Ltd.

The information within this guide does not represent the views of any third-party service or organisation.

CONTENTS

Hello and welcome to your guide: *IELTs General Training & Academic Study Practice Guide.* In this guide we will give you a full breakdown of EVERY SINGLE element of the IELTS assessment. We'll give you practice questions from both Academic and General Training, and a comprehensive outline of what both tests involve. Whichever test you are taking, by the end of our guide you will be in the perfect position to ace your assessment, and score 8+ marks.

So, without further ado, let's begin!

What is IELTS?

IELTS stands for International English Language Testing System. It is essentially a system which measures the language and writing proficiency of people who want to work or study in a country where English is the primary language. The scoring is done on a scale of 9, with 9 being the highest (at expert level) and 1 being the lowest (at non-user level).

There are two versions of the IELTS, which are as follows:

Academic. IELTS Academic is designed for candidates applying to higher education or professional registration.

General Training. IELTS General Training is designed for candidates migrating to the UK, Canada or Australia, or who are applying for secondary education or work experience/training in an environment where English is the primary language.

Both versions of the IELTS will assess your listening, reading, writing and speaking skills. The listening and speaking elements are the same for both tests, but the reading and writing elements will differ.

How This Book Is Structured

To make things easier for you, we've broken this book down into four sections. To begin with, we'll give you some top grammar and writing tips, which will make the tests a whole lot easier. Then, we'll cover the IELTS Academic, followed by IELTS General Training, and finishing with Speaking and Listening. This book contains hundreds of sample questions, so it's the perfect practice resource for anyone studying for their test. In every section, we'll explain exactly what the tests involve, and what type of questions you are likely to see.

As promised, we'll begin with some basic grammar and punctuation tips.

General Writing Tips

In English, punctuation consists of a number of symbols, marks, or signs which are deployed around letters and words, in order to convey the writer's intended meaning. The use of spacing also comes under punctuation. All the different punctuation marks perform different jobs within a sentence, all of which are important.

Punctuation is a good place to start when discussing writing, as it allows us to give meaning and form to our words and sentences. Without punctuation, comprehending writing of any length would be nigh on impossible. This is the point of punctuation – to aid understanding.

Another reason to begin by looking at punctuation is because its rules are mostly set in stone. For academic writing, personal style should not affect how you use punctuation – at least not too much. Each punctuation mark has its own specific use, which helps to convey a specific meaning within a sentence.

So, using different punctuation marks in different places within the same sentence will alter its meaning.

For example:

- *A woman, without her man, is nothing.*

- *A woman: without her, man is nothing.*

The full stop (.)

Of course, the main use of a full stop is to show where a sentence ends. The examples below are all 'complete' sentences, which are what you should be writing in.

For example:

- *American writer Mark Twain was born in Missouri.*

- *The tallest mountain in Ecuador is called 'Chimborazo'.*

- *The sale of vehicles represents the United Kingdom's second largest export.*

While this is simple, let's look now at what constitutes a complete sentence.

A complete sentence will always contain at least one main clause. A main clause will contain a subject as well as a verb to act on this subject.

Have another look at the example sentences used above. This time, you will find the subjects of the sentences highlighted, and the verbs of the sentences underlined.

- *American writer Mark Twain <u>was born</u> in Missouri.*

- *The tallest mountain in Ecuador <u>is called</u> 'Chimborazo'.*

- *The sale of vehicles <u>represents</u> the United Kingdom's second-largest export.*

If you are unsure as to whether a sentence you have written is incomplete, try to identify its subject(s) and verb(s). If you can't, you may not have written a complete sentence – you may have written a sentence fragment.

Examples of Sentence Fragments

- *Riding on the coattails of another's successes.*

- *To visit her friend on St. Patrick's Day.*

- *And went to Dudley for work experience.*

As you can see, the above 'sentences' do not show verbs acting on subjects – their subjects are implied. In the first one, we do not know *who* has been riding on the coattails. Therefore, the phrase is merely a sentence fragment. As a general rule, you should avoid using sentence fragments in your writing.

The comma (,)

The comma is a deceptively difficult piece of punctuation to use. For this reason, it is often misused and/or overused. The difficulty lies in the fact that there are many different writing situations that require the use of a comma, and many situations where its use would be incorrect.

So, we can say that there are many different types of comma.

The simplest use of the comma is to separate nouns in a list.

For example:

- *The government is prioritising education, health, and libraries.*

- *The new signing brings pace, power, and vision to the squad.*

- *Bleak House, Great Expectations, and Little Dorrit are all works by Charles Dickens.*

Note: The examples given above all employ the 'Oxford Comma' or 'serial comma' (a comma between the penultimate item in the list and 'and'), which is generally seen as being optional.

The Oxford Comma

Those in favour of the Oxford comma suggest it can bring clarity to certain situations. For example, consider the following two versions of this sentence:

- *'I love my children, Dracula, and Frankenstein.'*

- *'I love my children, Dracula and Frankenstein.'*

As you can see, the use of the Oxford comma in the first sentence makes it crystal clear that the writer loves their children, as well as the two characters of Dracula and Frankenstein. The other version of the sentence could suggest something rather different – that the writer's children *are* Dracula and Frankenstein.

As when listing nouns, commas are also used to separate listed adjectives and adverbs. Think about when you want to describe something with more than one word in a row. You'd use commas to separate these words!

For example:

- *The great, grey mountain peak stood ominously above the village.*

- *Move the rod slowly, precisely, and decisively if you want to catch a fish.*

- *The lavender plant is known for its fragrant, colourful, and attractive flowers.*

Another extremely common use of the comma is to separate clauses within sentences.

For example:

- *Ricardo bought a new pair of shoes, but did not get his watch repaired as intended.*

- *As the room filled with water, the family became more and more afraid.*

- *I've never watched musicals, and don't intend to start doing so now.*

While this type of comma might end up being the most commonly appearing one in your writing, make sure you use it correctly. In other words, beware the comma splice.

The Comma Splice

A comma splice occurs when a writer employs a comma to link two independent clauses – clauses that could make sense on their own as sentences. As shown above, a comma can be used to separate such clauses within one sentence, but with the use of other connective words like 'and' or 'but'. So, when a comma is used to separate two independent clauses (clauses that could make sense on their own as sentences), an error occurs.

For example (these are INCORRECT sample sentences):

- *A lioness's top speed is around 50mph, they can run fast in short bursts.*

- *I enjoy playing the piano, I use it to relax.*

- *The Battle of Maidstone took place in June 1648, it ended in victory for the parliamentarians.*

The problem with these sentences is that a comma is not sufficient to link them. The two clauses either need to be in their own sentences, or connectives/a different punctuation mark needs to be used. See below for correct versions of the three wrong examples given above. The highlighted areas show what has been changed to make the sentences correct.

- *A lioness's top speed is around 50mph; they can run fast in short bursts.*

- *I enjoy playing the piano. I use it to relax.*

- *The Battle of Maidstone took place in June 1648, and it ended in victory for the parliamentarians.*

Similarly, commas are also used to separate introductory parts of a sentence from its main clause.

For example:

- *After arriving home from the festival, Nathan fired up his computer.*

- *Despite initial disagreement, the deal was struck relatively quickly.*

- *Fortunately, there was not too much damage.*

A further use of the comma is to separate 'extra' details of a sentence from its main clause. In these cases, two commas would be used to contain the 'extra' information from the main content of the sentence. A good way to check if you are using this type of comma correctly is to take out the 'extra' information and see if the main clause makes sense by itself. If it does, you're looking good.

For example:

- *The beach, which was empty and serene, was her favourite place to spend time.*

- *Seoul's Olympic Park, which played host to the 1988 Olympics, was renovated in 2011.*

- *Rahul, my cousin, graduated from university this summer.*

Commas also have an important role to play when writing dialogue or direct speech. Namely, they are used to separate the direct speech from the rest of the sentence.

For example:

- *"It certainly is striking," he said, "but it's not my cup of tea."*

- *"I'm warning you," she whispered, "behave yourself or you're out of here."*

- *"As you can see," said the tour guide, "the area becomes quite different following a rainstorm."*

Note: The rules surrounding comma splices and direct speech are murky at best. In many situations, such as when writing novels, a comma splice as we've discussed is often not seen as a mistake – more of a stylistic choice. (See the second example above.) In academic writing, should it be relevant, it's probably best to err on the side of caution. Perhaps ask a teacher, tutor, or advisor about their preference on the matter!

The colon (:)

While the comma is deceptively difficult to use, the colon is deceptively easy. That is to say, its uses are relatively few and clear.

Firstly, its most simple use is to introduce listed nouns.

For example:

- *The ingredients are simple: milk, eggs, flour, and butter.*

- *There were myriad treasures underneath: precious stones, jewellery, coins, everything.*

- *She wrote down what was most important to her: her dog, her friends, and work.*

> Note: When using colons in this way, you should make sure that the introductory part of the sentence would make sense on its own. For example, you should NOT write – 'The ingredients are: milk, eggs, flower, and butter.' You would not need to use a colon in this case. So, the colon is not <u>required</u> for every situation to do with introducing lists, although it can add clarity and style.

Another prominent use of the colon is to reveal and develop themes and ideas within a sentence. While this sounds complicated, you'll see from the examples that it's actually quite simple.

For example:

- *There was one thing on his mind: vengeance.*

- *The coach was under no illusions: if he lost one more game, his career was over.*

- *The world is embroiled in an ongoing crisis: stagnating wages and soaring prices.*

This is most often done for emphasis.

Again, the part of the sentence that falls before the colon should make sense on its own. However, in creative writing, you may wish to flout this rule should it muscle in on your style too much.

The semicolon (;)

The semicolon is probably the most complained-about punctuation mark. Be it confused novices struggling to get to grips with it, or smug veterans maligning its misuse, you'll have heard people arguing about the semicolon.

In truth, it's not that interesting, or even that difficult to use.

Its main use is to separate two independent clauses that are closely related. This means that the two halves of the sentence must be able to make sense by themselves. In other words, your sentence containing the semicolon could feasibly be split into two perfect sentences.

However, the choice not to split them in this way, and instead employ a semicolon, would be a choice to emphasise a link of some sort between the two clauses.

For example:

- *Graham was easily frightened; the slightest noise could startle him.*

- *Audrey had a very specific taste in film; she would watch old comedies but nothing else.*

- *I'm karate mad; I train every day for at least 3 hours.*

Think back to the section about the comma splice – the semicolon could stand in for an erroneous comma in these situations.

Also, make sure that you are not using a semicolon where a colon would be more appropriate. In many situations, if what follows your semicolon could not make sense as its own sentence, a colon would be more appropriate.

However, in cases like this, it may be preferable to rewrite your sentence into two sentences, or use a comma and a connective!

For example:

INCORRECT:	In 1982, Mexico suffered a terrible tragedy; the eruption of El Chichón.
CORRECT:	In 1982, Mexico suffered a terrible tragedy: the eruption of El Chichón.
CORRECT:	In 1982, Mexico suffered a terrible tragedy. It was the eruption of El Chichón.

Note: See how 'It was' was added to the second part of the third example to create a second complete sentence.

Another use of the semicolon is to separate items in a list which are long or convoluted in some way. This is done to provide clarity and understanding where simply using commas would not have been sufficient.

For example:

- ***Belligerents of the War of the Roses included: Henry VI, House of Lancaster; Henry VII, House of Tudor; Margaret of Anjou, House of Valois-Anjou; and Edward IV, House of York.***

As you can see, using semicolons to separate the listed items here allows the use of the comma within the listed items themselves, and makes it clear the Houses belong with the respective rulers. It even has the use of an Oxford semicolon…

So, let's look at what this list would have looked like without the use of the semicolon:

For example (this is an INCORRECT sample sentence):

- ***Belligerents of the War of the Roses included: Henry VI, House of Lancaster, Henry VII, House of Tudor, Margaret of Anjou, House of Valois-Anjou, and Edward IV, House of York.***

This sentence is much more confusing; the reader has been led to believe that the Houses are separate from the rulers. The semicolon is the saviour of this situation.

The hyphen (-)

The hyphen (-) is another potentially tricky piece of punctuation to use correctly. It is often confused with the dash (–), its longer cousin. We'll cover the dash in the next section.

Despite potential hurdles, the hyphen has a clear set of rules surrounding its use. However, it can get complicated. Let's look at a few examples.

Hyphens are most often used within adjectives that are made up of two (or more) words and other compound words.

For example:

- ***Twenty-first century literature.***

- *An off-the-cuff remark.*

- *A self-diagnosed illness.*

However, it is easy to make mistakes and use hyphens when there is no need to. For example, if you wanted to use 'off the cuff' adverbially rather than as an adjective (describing a verb rather than a noun), then you should not use hyphens.

For example:

- *The remark was made off the cuff.*

Also, hyphens should not be employed in sentences where these types of adjectives follow the noun. In the first three examples above, they precede the noun.

For example:

- *The remark was off the cuff.*

- *The century was the twenty first.*

- *The illness was self-diagnosed.*   (*This is an exception! See below.*)

However, in a quirk of the language, the same is not true of compound words containing the word 'self', such as 'self-diagnosed'. When using this word following a noun, the hyphen stays.

For example:

- *The illness was self-diagnosed.*

- *They considered themselves to be quite self-sufficient.*

- *The archetypal villain is ruthless and self-serving.*

The dash (–)

The dash, often confused with the hyphen, is a completely different punctuation mark to its shorter counterpart. It serves an entirely different purpose within a sentence, and is in no way interchangeable!

The main use of the dash is to signal an 'interruption' within a sentence. This could be in the shape of a change of subject, theme, or tone. When writing dialogue, even, this could be a literal interruption!

However, in academic writing, the use of the dash would be a stylistic choice to represent a change of direction within a sentence, or to provide juxtaposition between two clauses in a sentence. Overall though, it's probably good advice to use the dash sparingly. See below for some examples of its use.

For example:

- *Edgar was set to become Earl of Gloucester and inherit his father's title — but Edmund had other ideas.*

- *Rules are rules, of course — yet they are made to be broken.*

- *She was shy, quiet, and unassuming — or so she'd have you believe.*

Another way the dash is used is similar to how commas that separate 'extra information' from main clauses of sentences are used. So, in these situations, you'd need to use a pair of dashes.

For example:

- *The beach — which was empty and serene — was her favourite place to spend time.*

- *Seoul's Olympic Park — which played host to the 1988 Olympics — was renovated in 2011.*

- *Rahul — my cousin — graduated from university this summer.*

While this usage of the dash seems interchangeable with the commas mentioned above, they convey a slightly different meaning or connotation. Namely, the choice to use dashes instead of commas in a situation like this would be the choice to write a more emphatic sentence.

In other words, if the 'extra information' you wish to include within your sentence is more important, or you wish to draw more attention to it, perhaps you'd prefer the use of dashes (over commas) to contain it. In creative writing, this is certainly something to experiment with. When writing dialogue, for example, a pair of dashes could be used when you wish your character to go off track in the middle of a sentence before resuming.

For example:

- *"I'm very angry with you — I'll deal with Maurice later — you're in so much trouble."*

- *"Mrs. Haverley is fully booked all week — I need to tell Mason, actually — please don't bother her."*

- *"As you can see, the River Nile stretches from — Jeff, stop talking — all the way down in Uganda, through the continent, and up into the Mediterranean Sea."*

However, in most situations, you should stick to using commas to separate extra information like this in a sentence. The use of dashes in this way could even be considered incorrect if the extra information does not represent a clear enough interruption of the sentence.

Crafting Sentences

Now that we've shown you how to craft a sentence, let's dive into what makes a 'good sentence', and what you should be aiming for when writing under formal conditions.

A good starting point would be to think about the length of your sentences. In many cases, you should aim to keep your sentences as short as possible. This is not for word count-related reasons, but to keep your sentences concise and focused. Essentially, it ensures you are not writing 'empty' sentences or waffling.

Of course, in creative writing, such a hard-and-fast rule could stymie your voice or stifle a particular mood that you were aiming to create. In these cases, don't let ruthless efficiency get in the way of your style.

So, let's have a look at how you can cut the excess words from your sentences.

For example:

- *Without question, it is possible to say that the Fool has an important role to play in the plot of King Lear. This character represents Lear's conscience throughout and, ironically, acts a foil to his foolishness.*

This could become:

- *The Fool represents Lear's conscience throughout and, ironically, acts as a foil to his foolishness.*

Avoiding repetition is an effective way to sharpen up a sentence; you don't need to say the same thing in many different ways. If you are writing an essay, repetition will not further your point or improve your work. It could even cause whoever's marking to lose interest or penalise you. You don't want to create the impression that you're fluffing up your writing to meet the word count – quite the opposite.

Make your reader feel as if every word was selected for a clear and proactive reason. If you're looking to cut down a piece of writing that's over the word limit, experiment with taking out words and phrases that could be considered as overkill. A lot of the time, you'll find that the meaning of what you're saying hasn't changed, and your writing has become punchier and more impactful.

Creating Paragraphs

In this section, we're going to look beyond creating sentences and look at how best to weave them together to craft paragraphs. Luckily, in academic or any sort of formal writing, there are clear rules you can follow to make sure that your paragraphs are concise, focused, and driving your point forwards. Read on for our tips on creating paragraphs.

Paragraph Structure

In academic writing or essay writing, it is extremely important to write good paragraphs. A good paragraph is one that is contained, and one that does not contain lots of complex points.

As a rule, you should try and keep paragraphs limited to one main point. This way, you can stop paragraphs from growing out of control, allowing the reader to understand your argument more easily.

A great way to make your paragraphs easier to follow is to treat each of them as a miniature essay. By this, we mean that each paragraph should have a short sentence which introduces the main point, followed by the point itself. Finally, you should end the paragraph with a short sentence which briefly summarises your point, and demonstrates how it relates to the question that you're answering. This way, you'll have your argument for each paragraph clearly laid out for the reader to see.

If it helps, you can try coming up with a subtitle for each paragraph in your essay. Don't include this in the finished copy, but writing each paragraph with the main point of it explicitly in mind will help you focus your efforts, and create a more consistent piece of work.

Once you have a paragraph structure laid out, the flow of your essay will become a lot more pronounced. This means that you'll be able to spot parts that feel disjointed and correct their course. By 'disjointed', we mean parts of the essay which either stick out from the flow of your essay and don't lead to any new points, or sections which actively move against the flow of your essay.

Imagine your essay is a river. Each part of the essay should flow into the next, as your argument cumulatively builds up towards the conclusion. The points made in earlier paragraphs should always contribute to later ones, and those which don't could be considered as irrelevant.

For example, if paragraphs A, B, C, and D all support a larger argument made in paragraph F, but the argument in paragraph E has no bearing on this argument, then you need to consider whether it's paying off for you. If the paragraph isn't benefitting your argument, then you should probably get rid of it and use the space to write something relevant.

There's no set length that a paragraph needs to be, but they can be too long. If you have a single paragraph that's significantly larger than the rest in your essay, it might be worth revisiting to see how it can be divided into smaller parts. This will prevent your essay from becoming 'bogged down'. Likewise, lots of tiny paragraphs can look too fragmented or poorly developed.

Academic Writing:
About the Test

IELTS Academic is designed for candidates who are applying to higher education or professional registration. There are four sections in total to the IELTS Academic Test. In this section we will cover the Academic Writing and Reading. The speaking and listening will be covered at the end of this book.

Let's start with IELTS Academic Writing.

IELTS Academic Writing

The IELTS Academic writing assessment is a comprehensive test of your writing skills. Just like the reading assessment, the exercises have been deliberately chosen to be appropriate for people applying for a university course or wanting professional registration.

The test will last for 60 minutes, and assesses elements such as:

- Your ability to write clearly and concisely.

- Your ability to accurately summarise data.

- Your ability to describe.

- Your ability to explain.

- Your ability to identify arguments, and respond to them.

- Your ability to write formally.

- Your ability to use language to persuade and inform.

- Your grasp of grammar, spelling and punctuation.

There are two tasks in the IELTS Academic writing assessment. The second task is the most important in terms of your writing band score, contributing to double that of task 1.

The tasks are as follows:

Task 1
In this task, you will be given a graph, table or chart. Your job is to look at the image and then summarise or explain the information that's being presented. You might also be given a diagram of a machine, or a device, and then asked to explain how it functions and how it works. The main aim of the assessment is to see how well you can identify important information and trends/patterns, whilst giving an overview of said information in an accurate and academic/formal style. Your main

priority should be to include the most important/relevant aspects of the image in front of you. You should try to include minor details if you can, but you will score higher if you focus on the more important elements of the image.

You will be given 20 minutes to complete this task. The aim should be to write 150 words in total. If you write any less than this then you will be penalised. You will not lose marks for exceeding the word count, but you should not spend any longer than 20 minutes on this task. You will also be penalised if you go off topic at any point during your written response, or you fail to adhere to basic requirements, such as sentence structure, grammar, spelling and punctuation. You must write in full and clear sentences, do not use bullet points or short-hand text.

When taking the test, you'll be provided with an answer booklet in which to write your responses.

Task 2
In this task, you will be given a topic and then asked to write about it in an academic/formal style. The topic will be given to you in the form of a prompt. For example, you might be given a statement which reads, 'Zoos are immoral and should be banned.' You'll then need to respond to this statement, either arguing for or against, with detailed analysis on why you believe what you believe. You should try to support your answer with evidence, and you are allowed to use examples based on your own personal experience. You must make sure that you focus on the statement in the question. For example, if the statement reads, 'Zoos are immoral, they should be banned,' then you need to focus your answer on zoos, not just on lions, or whatever your favourite animal is. While you could use the plight of some animals kept within zoos to strengthen your argument, this should not be the focus of your argument.

The minimum word count for this exercise is 250 words, and you will have 40 minutes to complete the assessment. Again, falling under the word count will result in you being penalised. The marks for task 2 are twice that of task 1, meaning that failure to complete this exercise will greatly harm your chances of scoring highly.

During this assessment, the main elements that are being tested are in relation to the fluency of your writing and vocabulary. You are also being tested on how well your response is structured, how well it uses persuasive language, and how well it cites information and ideas.

Basically, you need to put together a coherent and logical response, paying attention to grammar, spelling, and punctuation – all whilst addressing the main statement from the question.

Now that we've explained about the different elements of the test, let's move onto the really important stuff: how to pass!

Below we've provided you with some practice questions, so that you can get some idea of how to answer, before moving on to our real practice test.

Practicing IELTS Academic Writing

Practice Question 1

The graph below shows the relationship between shoplifting incidents and the time of year, in Scotland, Ireland and England.

Summarise the information by selecting and identifying the main features of the graph.

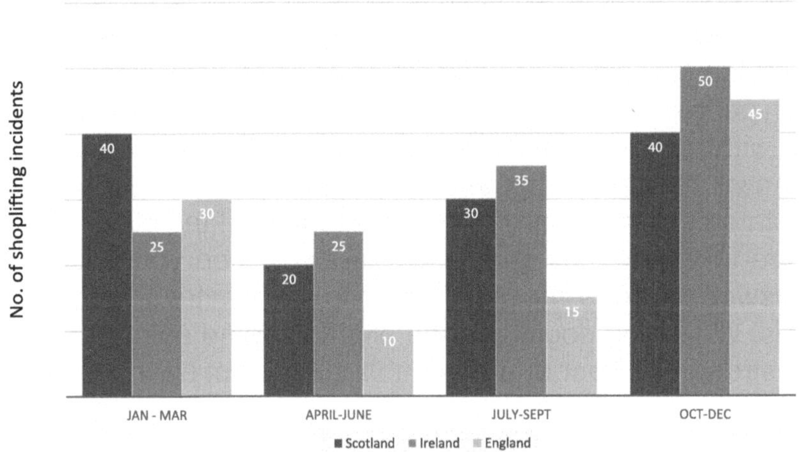

How To Answer

Sometimes, looking at a graph can seem quite intimidating. There's a lot of information to take in, and it can be quite hard to make sense of it all. The thing to do here is to stay composed. Don't panic and let the information overwhelm you. Take a moment just to look at everything in a calm and logical fashion, and work out exactly what the graph is showing. Once you've done that, your answer shouldn't be too difficult.

All you have to do is summarise exactly what you see in the graph, in 150 words or more.

So, how should we look at the above graph? The first thing that should stand out for you is that the graph shows the relationship between the months of the year and the number of shoplifting incidents that occurred, in the countries of Scotland, Ireland and England. Your first line should explain this. So:

'The graph shows a correlation between the time of the year and the number of shoplifting incidents that occur in the countries of Scotland, Ireland and England.'

Now that you've summarised the main point of the graph, you can move onto the actual data. When we look at this graph, we can clearly see that there are more shoplifting incidents occurring from January-March, and October-December, than there are from April-June and July-September. Therefore, logic would dictate that more shoplifting incidents are occurring during the colder months of the year.

Once you've established this, you just need to work out the numbers behind the increase/decrease, and then summarise this. Like so:

'By looking at this graph, we can see a clear indication that more shoplifting incidents occur during the 'colder' months of the year than during the hotter months. To demonstrate this, the graph shows that from January to March (in all three countries) there were 95 shoplifting incidents in total. This was followed by a marked decrease, with only 135 incidents occurring over the next 6 months. It is worth noting that there was an increase in shoplifting incidents from July till September, compared to April till June, but this was quite a minor leap.'

In the above we've covered the first 9 months of the year. Now we can close our summary by detailing the final 3 months of the year:

'Following this, and moving into the Autumn, we saw a large increase in the number of incidents – with 135 incidents occurring over the next 3 months, from October till December.'

If we put this altogether, we have a concise, accurate and 150+ word summary of the graph in question:

'The graph shows a correlation between the time of the year and the number

of shoplifting incidents that occur in the countries of Scotland, Ireland and England.

By looking at this graph, we can see a clear indication that more shoplifting incidents occur during the 'colder' months of the year than during the hotter months. To demonstrate this, the graph shows that from January to March (in all three countries) there were 95 shoplifting incidents in total. This was followed by a marked decrease, with only 135 incidents occurring over the next 6 months. It is worth noting that there was an increase in shoplifting incidents from July till September, compared to April till June, but this was quite a minor leap.

Following this, and moving into the Autumn, we saw a large increase in the number of incidents – with 135 incidents occurring over the next 3 months, from October till December.'

Now, let's look at another type of question, this time involving a diagram.

Practice Question 2

The diagram shows an ocean food chain. In your own words, describe this food chain and how it works.

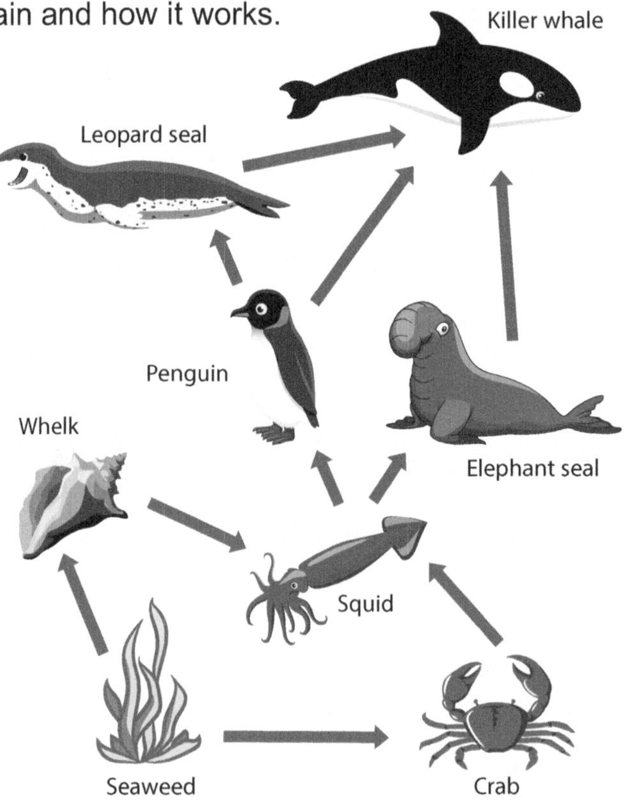

How To Answer

This is a very different type of question to the previous, in that it doesn't contain large amounts of data. However, there's still plenty of information here with which to construct a great response.

Just like before, let's start out by summarising exactly what we can see in the diagram:

'This diagram shows an aquatic food chain. In the diagram we can see a number of aquatic species, ranging from killer whales to squid.'

So, now that we've summarised the main point of the diagram, we can start exploring the details. This is quite a simple one – all you need to do is explain what eats what!

'The aquatic food chain shows which animals are higher and lower in the natural order of predator and prey. To start off with, we have seaweed. Seaweed is at the very bottom of the scale, and is consumed by both crabs and whelks. The next lowest creatures on the chain are the crab and whelk. Both the crab and whelk eat seaweed, but are consumed by squid. Squid have two main predators, the penguin and the elephant seal. The penguin is prey for the leopard seal, plus killer whales. Likewise, the elephant seal is also eaten by killer whales, who also consume leopard seals.'

Now, close out the summary with a conclusory statement:

'Based on the diagram, the killer whale is clearly the apex predator of this food chain. The killer whale does not have any predators.'

Put this all together, and we have a 152-word summary, that clearly and concisely explains what is happening in the diagram:

'This diagram shows an aquatic food chain. In the diagram we can see a number of aquatic species, ranging from killer whales to squid.

The aquatic food chain shows which animals are higher and lower in the natural order of predator and prey. To start off with, we have seaweed. Seaweed is at the very bottom of the scale, and is consumed by both crabs and whelks. The next lowest creatures on the chain are the crab and whelk. Both the crab and whelk eat seaweed, but are consumed by squid. Squid have two main predators, the penguin and the elephant seal. The penguin is prey for the leopard seal, plus killer whales. Likewise, the elephant seal is also eaten by killer whales, who also consume leopard seals.

Based on the diagram, the killer whale is clearly the apex predator of this food chain. The killer whale does not have any predators.'

Now let's do one more practice question, before we move onto some actual tests.

Practice Question 3

The table below shows the number of people who did sport, at school and university, and their gender.

Summarise the information by selecting and identifying the main features of the table.

Type of establishment	Secondary School		University	
	Male	Female	Male	Female
Football	256	62	398	162
Dance	165	268	169	368
Boxing	13	3	358	123
Tennis	98	68	160	76
Rounders	16	68	26	43
Total =	548	469	1111	772

Football = 878
Dance = 970
Boxing = 497
Tennis = 402
Rounders = 153

How To Answer

So, in this question instead of having a graph or a diagram, we now have a table, with the numbers and data filled in for us. Just like before, we need to start off the answer by summarising what the main point of the table is:

'The table shows the number of male and female athletes in secondary school, for 5 different sports, and then compares them against the number of male and female athletes at university, for the same sports.'

Now that we've summarised the main point of the table, we can move onto the smaller details – the numerical implications of the table.

'The table is broken down into individual sports – football, dance, boxing, tennis and rounders. It is also broken down to show how many of each gender participated in each sport. There are some clear differentials here, which show that certain sports are more popular amongst certain genders. For example, across both secondary school and university there were 654

boys who played football, compared to just 224 girls who played football. Both dance and boxing also contain large differentials, with dance weighted at 636 female participants to 334 male participants, and boxing weighted at 371 male participants to 126 female participants. The other sports, tennis and rounders, were more evenly spread.'

Sometimes, the table or data that you'll be given will contain lots of information. It would be impossible to summarise every single part of the above table in just 150 words, so your main aim should be to write as concisely as possible about the main elements of the table. In this case, we've identified the large differential between males and females in certain sports. However, you could also have identified the significant increase in the overall number of people who participated in sports at university, compared to that of secondary school, as the main point of the table.

Now, close out the summary with a conclusion:

'The table clearly indicates that there are certain sports which lean heavily towards male or female preference, whereas there are others which don't garner the same level of gender bias.'

Put this all together, and we have a 175-word summary, that accurately describes the table:

'The table shows the number of male and female athletes in secondary school, for 5 different sports, and then compares them against the number of male and female athletes at university, for the same sports.'

The table is broken down into individual sports – football, dance, boxing, tennis and rounders. It is also broken down to show how many of each gender participated in each sport. There are some clear differentials here, which show that certain sports are more popular amongst certain genders. For example, across both secondary school and university there were 654 boys who played football, compared to just 224 girls who played football. Both dance and boxing also contain large differentials, with dance weighted at 636 female participants to 334 male participants, and boxing weighted at 371 male participants to 126 female participants. The other sports, tennis and rounders, were more evenly spread.

'The table clearly indicates that there are certain sports which lean heavily towards male or female preference, whereas there are others which don't garner the same level of gender bias.'

Now that we've given you a good idea of how to tackle these types of exercises, it's time for you to have a go at some questions yourself.

In the next section we've included a range of sample questions, all similar to the above. This should give you plenty of practice!

Academic Writing:
Practice Test

Task 1

Q1. The table below shows statistics and figures for different brands of cars, with males and females. Summarise the information from the table in 150 words or more.

	Male				Female			
	18-25	26-35	36-49	50+	18-25	26-35	36-49	50+
Toyota	103	196	186	276	265	268	168	150
Ford	206	186	275	46	356	268	163	96
Mercedes	23	96	68	196	2	23	68	42
Renault	352	172	165	23	67	154	86	41
BMW	12	32	68	146	3	35	76	32
Vauxhall	269	126	112	136	109	120	162	106
Other	5	8	13	21	3	23	32	36
Total =	970	816	887	844	805	891	755	503

Grand total = 6471

Q2. The table below shows numerical figures for the route that male and female students took upon leaving school. Summarise the information from the table in 150 words or more.

	After students leave school...	
	Male	Female
College	15000	10000
University	26000	45621
Apprenticeship	9000	1236
Job	8523	6354
Total =	58523	63211

Q3. The table below shows the scores for students in English, Maths and Science examinations. Summarise the data in 150 words or more.

	Marks out of 40			
Subject	30 and above	20 and above	10 and above	0 and above
English	19	52	91	100
Maths	13	36	90	100
Science	11	42	87	100
AVERAGE	14	43	89	100

Q4. The image below shows conviction and crime rates for adults and people aged under 21. Summarise the information in 150 words or more.

	Convicted				Non-Convicted			
	Male		Female		Male		Female	
	A	U21	A	U21	A	U21	A	U21
Theft	166	265	68	96	46	26	24	15
Drug Offences	356	254	126	85	12	4	4	3
Motoring	369	369	49	109	56	65	31	45
Criminal Damage	256	251	169	56	43	15	2	13
Sexual Offences	235	96	19	10	5	3	2	1
Fraud	357	23	120	8	13	11	16	10
Total =	1739	1258	551	364	175	124	79	87

Grand Total = 4377

Convictions = 3912
Non Convictions = 465

Q5. The pie chart below shows the percentage of students in each GCSE subject at a local secondary school and the number of non-US students in the subject of Geography. There were 118 students total, in Geography.

Summarise the information in 150 words or more.

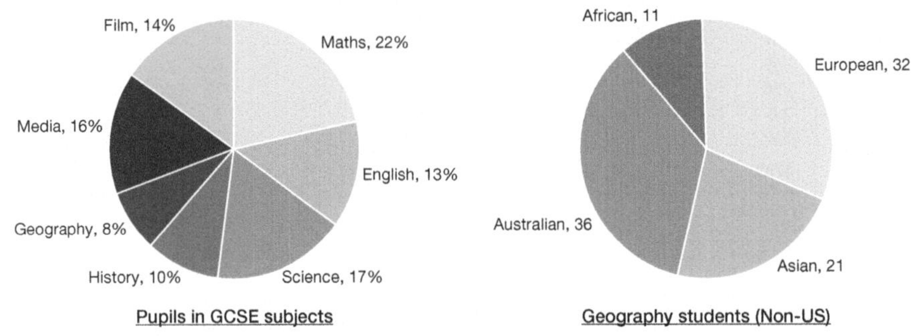

Pupils in GCSE subjects

Geography students (Non-US)

Q6. The image below shows the medical admission process, for patients with health problems.

Summarise the information in 150 words or more.

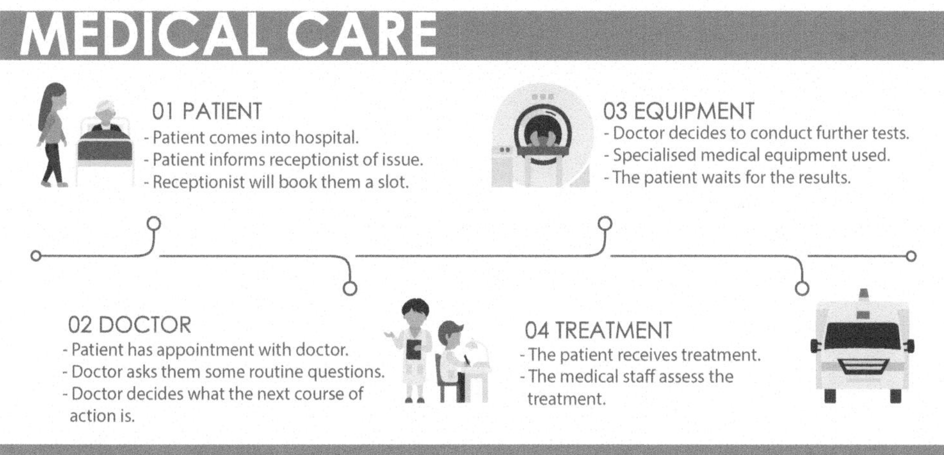

Q7. The image below shows information related to diabetes.

Summarise the information in 150 words or more.

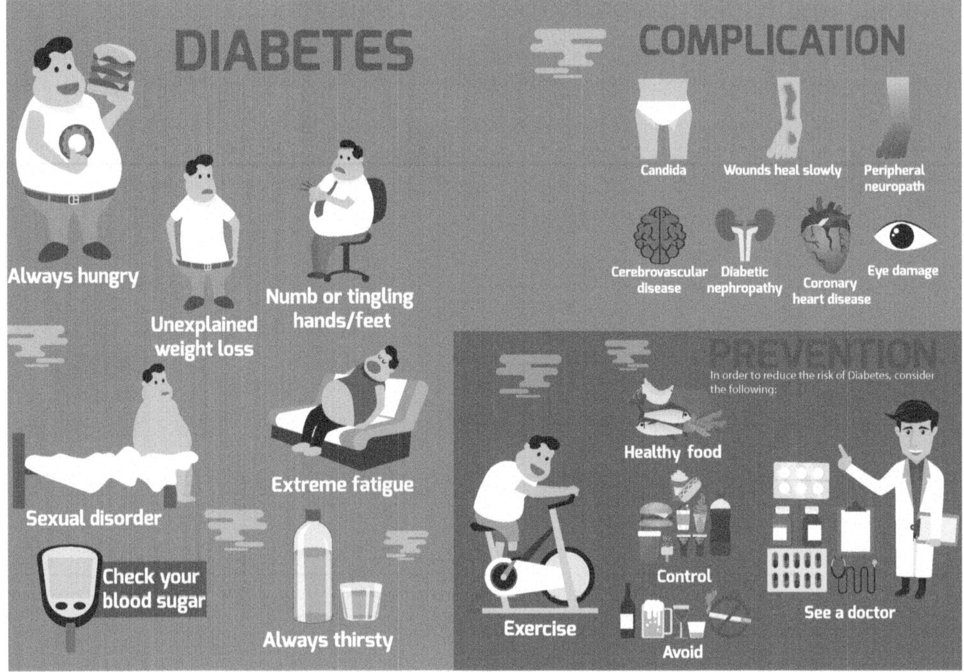

Q8. The image below shows important information about the justice system, and the components within this system.

Summarise the information in 150 words or more.

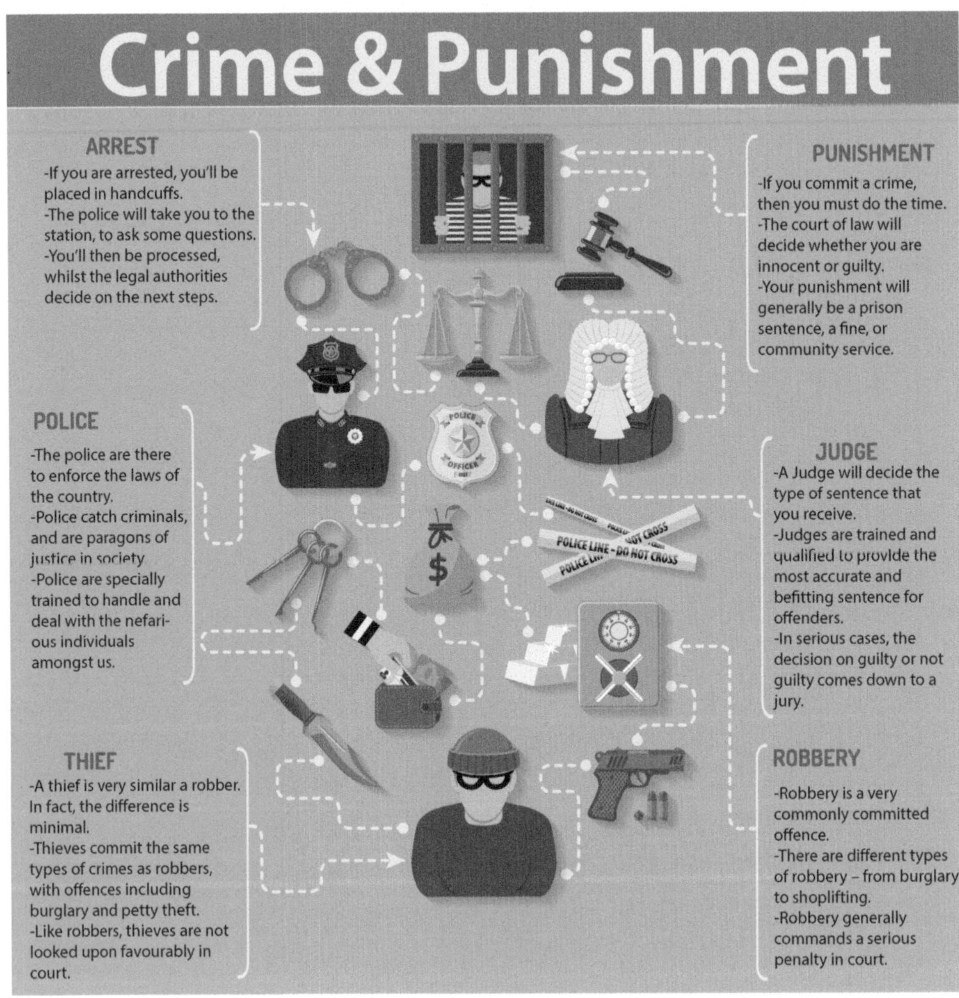

Q9. The image below shows the menu from a fancy restaurant. Summarise the information in 150 words or more.

Q10. The image below shows the impact that sport has upon the world. Summarise the information in 150 words or more.

Q11. The image below shows the role that intelligence agencies play in keeping public figures safe.

Summarise the information in 150 words or more.

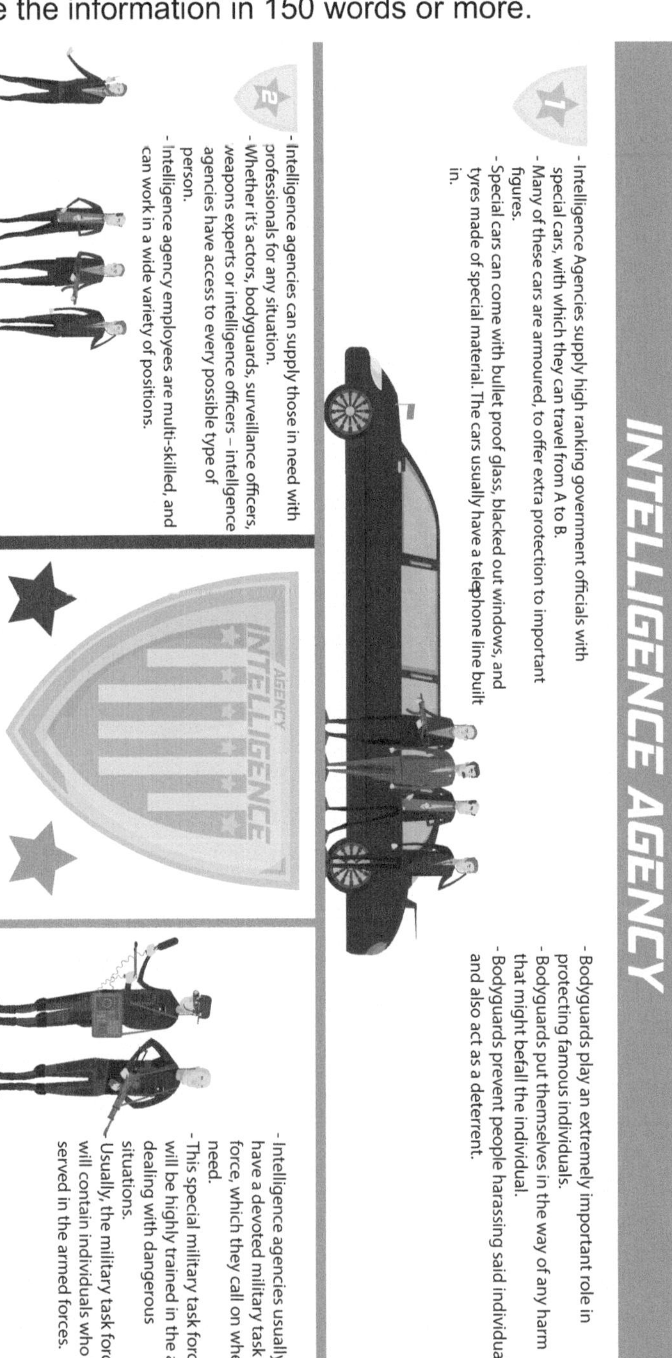

Q12. The image below shows some essential facts about obesity, and how to prevent it.

Summarise the information in 150 words or more.

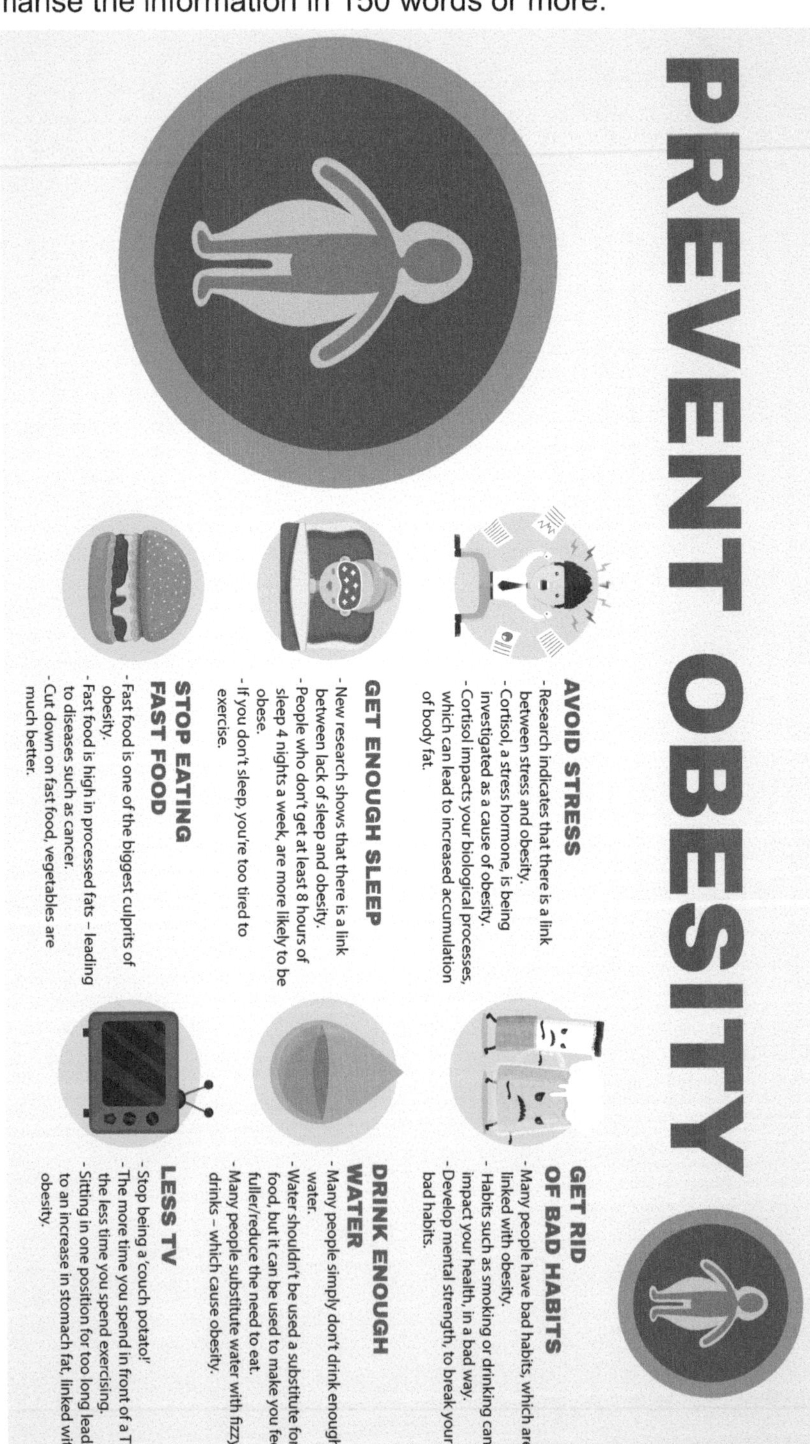

Q13. The diagram below shows a common food web. Describe this food web, in 150 words or more.

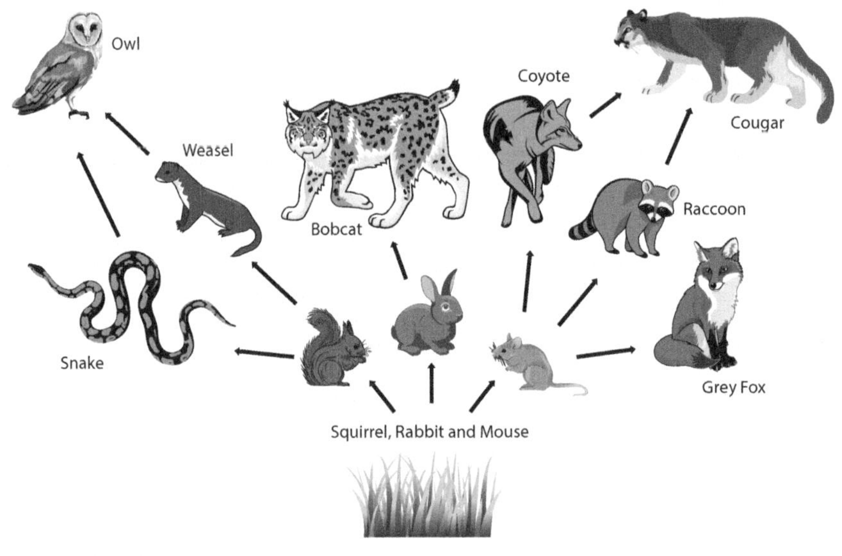

Q14. The diagram below shows a plant. Describe this diagram, in 150 words or more.

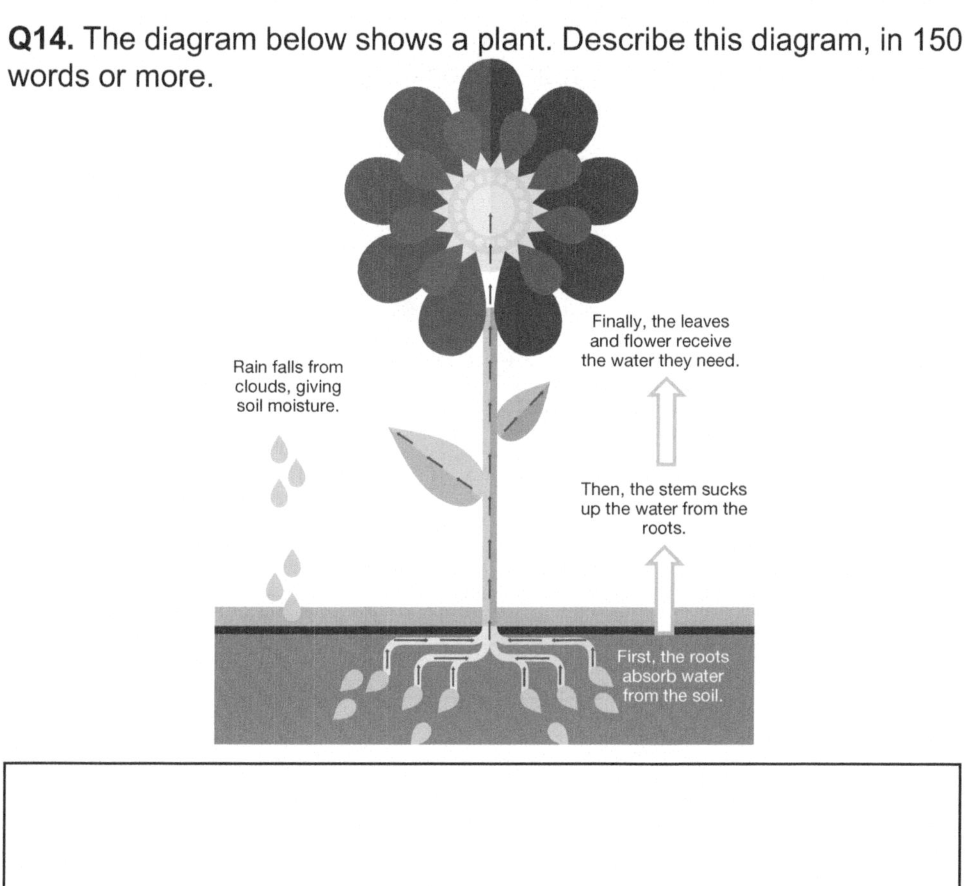

Q15. The table shows the number of English papers published by top UK universities over a six-year period. Summarise the data in 150 words or more.

Task 2

Q16. *'Prisoners should not be allowed to vote in elections.'*

Discuss whether you agree or disagree with the above statement, in 250 words or more.

Q17. *'Prostitution is treated too harshly, and should be legalised.'*

Discuss whether you agree or disagree with the above statement, in 250 words or more.

Q18. *'Music should be free for everyone. The government should legalise the practice of downloading music from websites such as YouTube.'*

Discuss the validity of the above statement, in 250 words or more.

Q19. 'UK schools should reintroduce corporal punishment. In the long term, this would be beneficial for children and their behaviour.'

Discuss the validity of the above statement, in 250 words or more.

Q20. *'Euthanasia is an appalling concept and should not be considered for legalisation.'*

Discuss whether you agree or disagree with the above statement, in 250 words or more.

Q21. 'School uniforms are a restrictive concept, and have no advantages versus allowing students to wear their own clothes.'

Discuss whether you agree or disagree with the above statement, in 250 words or more.

Q22. *'Darts is unfairly maligned, and should be considered an Olympic Sport.'*

Discuss whether you agree or disagree with the above statement, in 250 words or more.

Q23. 'The death penalty is an appalling and barbaric concept. It should stay abolished.'

Discuss whether you agree or disagree with the above statement, in 250 words or more.

Q24. *'Abortion is immoral and should not be given legal status in the UK.'*

Discuss whether you agree or disagree with the above statement, in 250 words or more.

Q25. *'It doesn't matter if certain species become extinct. There are plenty of other species well equipped to step into the gap.'*

Discuss whether you agree or disagree with the above statement in 250 words or more.

Answers to IELTS Academic Writing

Q1.

The table in question shows the popularity of certain brands of car, with males and females, from the ages of 18-50+.

There are 7 car brands in total: Toyota, Ford, Mercedes, Renault, BMW, Vauxhall, and other. By looking at the table we can clearly see that 'other' is the least popular choice, by a significant margin, with just 141 people from both gender categories and all of the age ranges selecting this. The table itself raises some interesting data patterns. The most popular car choice amongst men was Toyota, with 761 men selecting this. In contrast, the most popular car choice for women was Ford...albeit there was only a difference of 32 selections between this and Toyota. Toyota and Ford were the overwhelming favourites in terms of selection, with 1612 people across all ages and genders choosing Toyota, and 1596 people across all ages and genders choosing Ford.

When looking at the table, we can see that the most popular age and gender bracket for cars in general was male, 18-25, whereas the least popular age and gender bracket for cars was female, 50+.

Q2.

The table in question shows figures for the route that male and female individuals took upon leaving school. The table shows whether males and females attended college or university, or whether they got a job or an apprenticeship following their education.

The first thing that we should be able to notice when looking at this table is that there were a huge number of females who went to university following school — 45621 in total. This figure dwarfs any other in the table, with the closest being males who went to university, with 26000 respectively. By far the least popular option (for everyone surveyed) was the apprenticeship route — and this is demonstrated by the fact that only 1236 females took this up, which is the smallest figure in the whole table. Although apprenticeships were more popular with males than getting a job, overall there were just 10236 apprenticeships in total, compared to 14877 people who got a job.

Q3.

In this results-based table we can see examination scores for 100 pupils, in English, Maths, and Science. When looking at this table, the first thing we should notice is that the highest test score figures were achieved in

English. In English, 19 pupils achieved a score of 30/40 or higher. Likewise, there were 52 pupils who achieved a score of 20/40 or higher. There was very little to separate Maths and Science. Whilst Maths outscored Science in the top bracket by just two pupils, with 13 Maths students achieving 30/40 or higher, compared to Science's 11 students achieving 30/40 or higher, there were more students in Science who achieved 20/40 or higher — with 42 in total for Science and 36 for Maths. This means that, overall, students in both Maths and Science performed almost equally well, but students' scores in these subjects were some distance behind their scores for English.

Q4.

The table in question shows statistics for the number of males and females who were convicted of certain crimes. There are 6 crimes listed in total, and the people listed are broken down into the following categories: Adult male, under 21 male, Adult female, under 21 Female, Convicted and Non-Convicted.

The first thing that should stand out when looking at this table is that the number of people convicted absolutely dwarfs the number of people who were not convicted. There are 3912 convictions, to just 465 non-convictions. In terms of gender there is quite a differential too. The only categories where male survey participants did not outnumber female was in theft and motoring offences, with all of other categories displaying a clear numerical sway towards men.

In terms of age, there was a clear numerical bias towards adults, who committed (regardless of conviction or non-conviction) 2544 crimes to 1833 crimes committed by people under the age of 21.

Q5.

The pie chart below shows the percentage of students in each GCSE subject at a local secondary school and the number of non-US students in the subject of Geography.

When looking at these pie charts, we should be able to spot that the most popular subject overall is Maths. Maths received 22% of the votes, in comparison to the next highest subject, which was Science with 17%. The lowest scoring subject was Geography — with just 8%.

Geography is the topic of the second pie chart, which shows the number of non-US students taking the subject. There were 118 students total in

Geography, and 100 non-US students, meaning that non-US students made up approximately 85% of the total number.

The most common nationality in this chart was Australian, with 36 people in this category. There were 32 Europeans, and 21 Asians. The lowest scoring nationality in this chart was African, with just 11 people.

Q6.

This image shows the process that medical patients go through, when they encounter a health issue.

In step 1, the patient goes into the hospital. The first person they speak to is the hospital receptionist. After taking their details, the receptionist enquires with the patient as to what the problem is. Depending on the severity of the issue, the receptionist will then assign the patient an appointment slot. Following this, in step 2, the patient has their appointment with the doctor. In order to ascertain what the issue is, and how it could be fixed, the doctor asks the patient some routine questions, before deciding on the next steps.

In step 3, the patient is required to have further examination. This is done using specialised hospital equipment. Following this, the patient must wait for the results, before anything else can be done. Finally, in step 4, the patient receives treatment for the issue. The medical staff will assess how well the treatment is working. If it works well enough, the patient will be cured and healthy again.

Q7.

The image in question shows a diabetes infographic. The infographic focuses on the symptoms and complications of diabetes, as well as ways to prevent it.

To start out with, we have the symptoms. There are a wide variety of symptoms listed in this image. The first symptoms are linked to weight — always being hungry, and unexplained weight loss. The infographic also shows that sexual disorders, and having numb hands and feet, are symptoms of diabetes. The final two symptoms are extreme thirst and fatigue. The infographic advises you to check your blood sugar, if you are concerned.

Secondly, we have the complications arising from diabetes. These are plentiful, and incorporate candida, and brain and heart diseases. The *image shows that diabetes sufferers can also be prone to eye damage, and that their wounds may heal slower than someone without diabetes.*

Thirdly, we have the prevention methods. The infographic shows that the best way to combat diabetes is through regular exercises, and controlling your intake of foods that are low in nutrition, such as burgers or hotdogs. It recommends avoiding alcohol and smoking, and that you should make regular visits to a doctor.

Q8.

The image shows key information about crime and punishment, and the various individuals involved in the justice system.

To start out with, we have arrest itself. The act of arresting someone involves placing them in handcuffs, then taking them to the police station. Following this, the suspected criminal will then be processed, whilst the relevant legal bodies decide on what to do next. The next item on the list is police. As the image explains, the role of the police is to ensure that the laws of the country are kept to. They have special training in order to make competent at this, and following their training they will catch criminals, who do not obey the law.

On the opposite end of the spectrum, we have a thief. A thief commits crimes, such as burglary and petty theft. Generally, when a thief is brought into court to be tried, the court will not look favourably on this person. Next along from thief, we have robbery. Robbery is a type of crime, and is a very common offence. The image explains that robbery can consist of crimes such as burglary and shoplifting, and that perpetrators will be punished heavily in court.

After this, the next item is judge. A judge is a qualified professional, who decides what type of sentence offenders will receive. In the most serious of cases, judges are required to deliver the length of sentence only – as a jury will decide on the guilty or not guilty verdict.

Finally, we have punishment. As the image explains, people who commit crimes will be punished by the law, usually with a prison sentence, a fine, or community service.

Q9.

This image shows a menu from a restaurant. There are three categories on the menu: Starters, Main Course, and Desserts.

For a starter, visitors to the restaurant can choose between three options. The first option is smoked salmon. The smoked salmon is served with garlic, and comes with either vegetables or hollandaise sauce. The second option is garlic mushrooms. The mushroom are deep fried, and served with minty sauce. Customers can choose between portions of 6 or 9. The final starter is garlic bread. The garlic bread is imported direct from Naples, and is freshly toasted.

For the main course, again there is a choice of three options. The first option is spaghetti. The spaghetti is made with an extra special ingredient, and comes with Bolognese sauce. This is listed as one of the most popular items. Next, we have crispy shrimp. The shrimp are freshly caught by the restaurant's fishing team, no later than two days in advance. Finally, there is the BBQ burger. The burger comes with three slices of cheese and bacon, and the meat is imported from Spain and Italy.

For dessert, there are two options. Customers can choose between a cheesecake, which comes in chocolate, strawberry or vanilla flavour, or a chocolate fudge Sunday — which consists of chocolate flavoured cream, chocolate sprinkles, wedges, ice cream and syrup.

Q10.

The infographic highlights the importance of sport to the world, and lists various different types of sports.

To start out with, the infographic lists the benefits of sports in general, explaining that sport serves as a universal language, and unites people of different nationalities. The infographic gives special mention to the football World Cup.

Following this, the infographic talks about certain sports specifically, starting with motorsport. Motorsport is one of the most popular forms of global entertainment, and millions of people watch it every single year. Two of the most popular forms of motorsport are F1 and Moto GP.

Next, we have football. Football is the most popular sport in the entire world, and consequently is the most profitable too. International tournaments are held every two years, and the sport turns over billions of pounds year on year.

Basketball is the third sport on the list. Basketball is particularly popular in the USA, which has a billion-dollar national league, but it's played around the world. Basketball has given rise to superstars like Michael

Jordan, who are revered in the USA.

Finally, we have darts. Darts has seen a huge increase in popularity over the past ten years, but is most popular within the UK. The prize money for darts players is very high, with winners earning millions of pounds.

Q11.

The infographic explains the role that intelligence agencies play in keeping public figures safe.

The first image focuses on transportation and vehicles, plus bodyguards. Intelligence agencies provide high ranking figures with special cars, which are designed to protect the occupants from attack. The cars are often armoured, and come with bullet proof glass, blacked out windows and special tyres. Many of them also have a telephone built in, for emergency calls.

Many high ranking officials are assigned a bodyguard by the intelligence agencies. The role of a bodyguard is to shield these officials from harm, and prevent people from harassing them.

In the second image, we can see that intelligence agencies have a wide variety of professionals at their disposal. Intelligence agencies are able to provide public figures with access to actors, bodyguards, surveillance officers and weapons experts. Their employees have many skills and can work in many different positions. Following on from this, the image shows that intelligence agencies often have their own military task force, who are trained in dealing with dangerous situations. It is common for the professionals within this task force to have served in the armed forces, prior to employment.

Q12.

The image focuses on obesity, and how people can prevent this from occurring. There are six methods.

The first way to avoid obesity, is to avoid stress. The image explains that stress is a factor in obesity, since cortisol (a stress hormone) can impact human biological processes. This leads to an accumulation of body fat.

The second way to avoid obesity, is to ensure that you get enough sleep. Research indicates that people who don't get at least eight hours of sleep, for four nights of the week, are more prone to suffer from obesity. Furthermore, the image draws a link between tiredness and lack *of exercising.*

The third and fourth items on the list are linked – avoiding consumption of fast food, and getting rid of bad habits. Fast food is extremely high in processed fat, and can lead to deadly diseases such as cancer. Vegetables are a much healthier alternative. Other poor habits include smoking and drinking, which are linked with obesity.

The fifth item encourages you to drink more water. This can make you feel fuller/reduce the need to eat, plus water and staying hydrated are very important. The more water you drink, the less fizzy drinks you'll consume – reducing the risk of obesity.

Finally, the last item on the list is a TV. The image encourages the viewer to stop being a couch potato, i.e. stop sitting in front of a TV, get out and start exercising. Sitting in one position for too long leads to an increase in stomach fat, with is linked with obesity.

Q13.

The diagram shows a complex food web, with multiple top apex predators, and several mid-level predators.

At the bottom of the chain we have grass. This is consumed by the squirrel, rabbit, and mouse. All three of the aforementioned are prey to a number of animals, both mid-web predators and apex predators alike. The squirrel is eaten by the snake and the weasel, both of which are consumed by the owl. The rabbit is eaten by the bobcat – which has no predators. The mouse is eaten by the coyote and the racoon, both of which are eaten by the cougar. The cougar has no predators, and is therefore an apex predator. Likewise, the mouse is also prey to the grey fox, which also has no predators.

In total, there are 4 apex predators in this web: the owl, the bobcat, the cougar and the grey fox. There are only 3 animals in the entire web who would not be considered predators – the squirrel, the rabbit and the mouse.

Q14.

This diagram shows how plants use water for nourishment, and how this helps them to grow and blossom.

The first stage in the process occurs when it rains. Rain from the clouds falls onto the ground, which provides the soil with moisture. The soil absorbs this moisture, which is then carried into the earth below the plant. A plant has multiple roots, which extend deep below the ground. These roots take the moisture from the soil, passing it on to the stem. The stem serves as a safe passage for the water, which is then passed onto the leaves. It is also passed onto the flower. The diagram indicates the way in which this is done via a series of arrows, showing the direction that the water travels in once it has been absorbed by the roots of the plant. In this diagram we can see a healthy, blooming flower – which indicates that it has received a good supply of water.

Q15.

This table displays the quantity of English papers that were published by 5 UK universities, from 2000 until 2005.

The first thing we should notice about this table, is that there is no apparent overall trend for the rate at which papers are being published. From 2000 to 2001 there was an increase of 25 papers published annually, and this decreased in 2002. From 2002 onwards there was an increase in the numbers of papers published, but 2003-2005 saw roughly the same numbers of papers being published in each of the 3 years.

In terms of individual university trends, the highest publishing university over the 6-year period was Kings College, and the lowest publishing university over the 6-year period was Cambridge – who published just 10 papers in 2002 (joint lowest with East Anglia). Kings College led the pack by some distance, publishing in advance of 40 more English papers than the nearest competitors – Oxford and East Anglia.

Q16.

I strongly disagree with the above statement. I feel that there are a number of facets which make this argument incorrect, both logically and morally.

Firstly, I believe that not allowing prisoners to vote constitutes a violation of human rights. The reality is that these people have been imprisoned for two reasons a) to protect the public and b) as part of a rehabilitation service. Denying prisoners the right to vote does not protect the public, and directly contradicts the latter. Prisoners are still members of society and citizens of the nation, and therefore have the right to civil liberties.

In line with the above point, we live in a democratic society. This is a society which takes pride in the participation of all its people in the political process; regardless of how much money they have, their gender, their sexual orientation or class. By denying prisoners the right to represent themselves on a political level, we are contradicting the democracy that Western civilisation uses as its trump card.

Finally, I believe that keeping prisoners as part of the democratic process will increase their chances of adjusting back into civilian life. By not allowing them to vote, we are disenfranchising prisoners from society, reducing their sense of self-worth and increasing their bitterness towards those who have imprisoned them in the first place.

In conclusion, I feel that allowing prisoners to vote will have a multitude of benefits – and would fit more into the idea of prison as a 'rehabilitation' service, rather than one which aims to punish prisoners outright.

Q17.

I agree with the above statement. I feel that there are a number of sociological factors to take into account, all of which demonstrate that prostitution should indeed be legalised.

First of all, I believe it's fair to say that criminalising the act of prostitution puts those who work in the industry at risk. Instead of pushing people away from participating, it simply pushes them underground and heightens the risk of doing so. Sex workers are a frequent target for criminals. This is due to the fact that they are working in an illegal industry, so crimes often go unreported. Violators can take direct advantage of sex workers without fear of punishment or arrest. By making prostitution illegal, you reduce the safety barriers for individuals who depend on it to make a living.

Next, I would argue that having a legal, functioning sex market serves a positive purpose in society. It is arguably extremely outdated to criminalise the sex market. Many adults now take great satisfaction from non-marital sex and have varying reasons for why they might pursue this from a sex worker. Whether this is for companionship, fantasy fulfilment or comfort; people should have the right to engage in relations with each other, regardless of whether it involves a financial transaction or not.

Thirdly, you could argue that legalising prostitution would bring about positive changes for the industry, which would significantly benefit the workers. The fact that prostitution is illegal means that those who are in charge of selling sex workers to customers have a (often illegal) autonomy over their workers, and can use harmful measures/pressure tools to persuade them into taking a job that they don't want to do. Legalising prostitution would mean that the industry was more regulated, and incidents like this wouldn't take place.

In conclusion, I believe that there would be a number of benefits to legalising prostitution, namely that legalising prostitution would have significant benefits to those working within the industry – who are being placed at risk by the current laws.

Q18.

I strongly disagree with the above statement. I do not believe that music should be given this treatment, and I feel that the practice of downloading music from websites (without paying) is extremely harmful.

First of all, we must consider the impact that such behaviour has on the artists. By illegally downloading their music from the internet, you are bypassing the option to pay them for their services. Thus, you are acquiring a completely free product, with no benefit for the person who provided it to you. You would not walk into a shop and simply take something from the shelves, so why would it be considered acceptable to steal music? Music artists are people, just like anyone else, trying to make a living. By stealing their music, you are effectively putting your hand in their pocket.

Secondly, as mentioned, this practice is harmful. It's harmful not only to the artists, but to the music industry as a whole. The bottom line is this: the money that you pay for music goes towards more music. Therefore, on a basic level, by paying for music you are essentially putting an investment towards more content that you enjoy. If everyone took their music from the internet instead of paying for it, then both the quality of music as a whole and the number of songs released/artists would dwindle – which would ultimately harm everyone.

In conclusion, I believe that the practice of taking music from the internet is fundamentally negative and is not something the government should consider legalising. Music thieves are harmful to the industry, and to artists as a whole.

Q19.

I strongly disagree with the above statement. I feel that reintroducing corporal punishment into UK schools would have a profoundly negative impact, and is definitely not something we should be endorsing. The reasons I believe this are as follows:

Firstly, you could argue that corporal punishment would have a long term, negative effect on children. On a psychological level, being hit is extremely unsettling. Not only is it painful and humiliating, but it causes long lasting resentment towards those who have administered the punishment – in this case authority and the educational system. This would be harmful for the educational system, as it would foster a generation of children who grow up believing that they have been unfairly treated.

As human beings, we have outgrown the idea that hitting someone is the right way to enforce authority. In the UK, smacking is seen as abhorrent. Very few parents deliver physical punishment as a means of correcting behaviour. Part of the reason for this is that we are trying to set a good example for the next generation. By enforcing the idea on children that smacking is right, we would be setting a terrible precedent for the future. We would be teaching them that violence is the way to resolve issues.

Thirdly, you could argue that corporal punishment would significantly damage the relationship between students and their teacher, making it impossible to learn. Particularly with young children and teenagers, there needs to be a level of respect and trust established between the pupils and teacher, in order to maintain a harmonious learning environment. Corporal punishment would significantly detract from this. Students need to feel safe in the learning environment. By inducing an atmosphere of fear and pain, you create a situation where students are receiving negative reinforcement. Positive reinforcement has been shown as the best way to learn, and therefore corporal punishment would massively detract from the education system.

In conclusion, I feel that corporal punishment would bring about significant harm to UK schoolchildren. It is barbaric, outdated and should not be considered, under any circumstances.

Q20.

I disagree with the above statement. I strongly feel that euthanasia is something that should be legalised. The reasons I believe this are as follows:

Firstly, I believe that people should have a choice. As per human rights, they should be able to choose when to end their life. Just as they have a *right to live, they have a right to die. Provided this does not bring physical harm to any other citizen, it is unfair to force people to live if they do not want to. People should be given autonomy and control over their own future.*

Secondly, I think it is worth considering that there are worse things than death. For many people, living a life where an illness is slowly destroying their mind, their organs are failing or they are hooked up to artificial support; is equal to a second-rate existence. Many of these people would rather die than live like this, in unimaginable pain and suffering. It could be argued that it is far more humane to allow people in this state to choose their own death, than force them to go through even more pain and suffering, all the while knowing that they will die anyway.

Thirdly, you could argue that legalised euthanasia would improve the economy. By giving sufferers the choice to end their own lives, you would reduce the cost and time spent by the NHS who are ultimately trying to comfort and support patients who don't actually want to be alive. Very often, the medication that is assigned to deal with these issues or prolong a sufferer's life, will leave them in a state of delirium or even worse pain than before. End of life medication is not designed to save people. It is extremely expensive and often leads to worse suffering.

In conclusion, I believe that legalising euthanasia would be a good thing, and would make perfect sense from a moral, economical and human rights standpoint.

Q21.

I largely disagree with the above statement. I strongly feel that there are lots of benefits to the implementation of school uniforms, and that they are ultimately a positive thing. The reasons I believe this are as follows:

Firstly, you could argue that having a uniform encourages discipline. Just as you would set rules for children to abide by, in order to encourage order, you would set out a uniform as a code of conduct. Wearing a uniform serves as a useful symbol to children of the rules and regulations of their school. It's a great reminder that they need to stay behaved and uphold the values of the institution.

Secondly, you could argue that children don't have the maturity to choose clothing that is appropriate for the school environment. They are at a rebellious age, particularly in their teens, and giving them the choice of what to wear to school could have negative consequences.

Linking in with the above, it could be argued that allowing children to wear their own clothes to school will detract from their learning. Schoolkids and teenagers are at a vulnerable age, where they should be focusing on their education. Allowing them to wear their own clothes gives them another thing to think and worry about. Having a uniform also means that schools reduce the chances of bullying. Schoolchildren are competitive, and there is a danger that certain individuals will be singled out for their choice of clothing, leading to conflict and distress.

In conclusion, I believe that school uniforms are fundamentally a positive concept, and brings lots of benefits – for children and school's alike. They encourage a sense of unity, and reinforce the idea that the school rules and regulations are something to be respected and kept to.

Q22.

I am in full agreement with the above statement, and I believe that there is no defining quality which means that darts should not be considered for the Olympics. The reasons I believe this as are follows:

Firstly, it is arguable that disregarding darts comes down to pure snobbery. It's incorrectly assumed that some sports are better than others because of how much running or physical exercise their participants incur. Can we use this to objectively rank the sports? Is football more of a sport than volleyball because it requires more energy? Must we use physical exertion as a means of defining what is a sport, and what isn't?

Secondly, like art, there's no clear way of defining what constitutes a sport and what doesn't. This leaves us with the issue of deciding what counts as a sport and what doesn't. In turn, what should constitute an Olympic sport? Without any objective guidance, we must rely on completely subjective standards for defining sports at an Olympic level. The closest to an objective metric that we have is demand. The more demand there is for a sport to be shown at the Olympics, the more it should be considered. If people want darts to appear at the Olympics, they need to make their voices heard.

Ultimately, darts should be made into an Olympic sport because it would bring an element of realism to the games. The sports at the Olympics are for the elite, such as gymnastics. What the Olympics need are more sports that the everyday person can enjoy. By refusing to show a range of sports that meet various types of people's tastes, the Olympics exposes itself as an event purely for the rich and affluent.

Q23.

Currently, the death penalty is not used in the UK. I firmly believe that it should stay this way, and agree with the statement. The reasons I believe this are as follows:

Firstly, you could argue that the death penalty works as a deterrent in theory, but not in practice. Despite the penalty being used in the USA, there are still thousands of murders and serious crimes being committed. The death penalty has not stopped people from committing such crimes.

Secondly, you could argue that prison is in fact a much more serious sentence than the death penalty. Yes, we would be ending the lives of criminals, but this is a fairly quick experience. Prison is a more fitting punishment for murderers, as they are locked up for the rest of their life without little to no access to their family, in a dangerous and intimidating environment.

There is also the issue of morality. Surely, by murdering criminals, we are no better than them? Society has a responsibility to take a higher moral position than people such as this, and introducing the death penalty would be in direct conflict with this. It could be argued that if we introduce such a punishment, we are no better than those whom we are inflicting it upon.

Lastly, there is the question of what happens if we are wrong. There are numerous instances of people being found guilty, before new evidence comes to light that reverses the decision. If we execute someone, and it's later found out that they weren't guilty, how will society deal with this? How will the family of the convicted deal with this?

Q24.

I strongly disagree with the above statement. On a moral level, I think the speaker is totally incorrect. The reasons I believe this are as follows:

Firstly, a foetus cannot exist independent of its mother. It is attached via the placenta and umbilical cord, its health is completely dependent on the mother's health. This means that it cannot be seen as a separate entity, and therefore the mother should have the choice as to whether to abort it.

Secondly, you could argue that the world is extremely hypocritical about how it terms the word 'murder' in relation to abortion. Fertilized eggs that are used for IVF are regularly discarded, but this is not seen as murder. If this isn't the case, then how can abortion be murder? Likewise, the medical implications of abortion are often drastically exaggerated by pro-life campaigners. In reality, medical abortions have a 0.5% chance of inflicting serious medical damage on the woman, and are extremely safe.

Thirdly, if a woman has been forced into sex, and becomes pregnant as a result, is it really right to make her keep the baby? It's true that woman can have the morning after pill, but in instances like this many women are too traumatised to think logically. They shouldn't be punished for this.

Finally, some women are simply not at the right stage of their life to have a child. Whether they don't have the time, money or maturity to look after a baby, it would be a negative thing to bring a baby into the world when it cannot be properly looked after.

Q25.

I believe that the above statement is fundamentally wrong on a number of levels. Any species becoming extinct will have a major impact. The reasons for this are as follows:

Firstly, we must look at the impact that the extinction of a species has on the ecosystem as a whole. If we eliminate one species from the food chain, this can have unpredictable and dangerous consequences. For example, organism A gets eaten by organism B, and organism B gets eaten by organism C. If you remove organism A from the food chain, then organism B will lose its source of food and could die out, which in turn will have the same impact on organism C. On the other hand, organism B could start eating elsewhere, having an impact on another food chain. Thus, you can see how the extinction of a species has extremely far reaching consequences for many other species too.

Secondly, we must look at this question from a moral perspective. It isn't a case of whether it 'matters', it is a case of right and wrong. We would have a fundamental issue with someone who claimed that the human race needed to be made extinct, therefore we should take the same attitude towards other organisms on our planet.

Furthermore, the extinction of a certain species would have a significant impact on a number of people too. All around the world, there are specific conservation groups set up for every single animal. Whether it's tigers, bears, lions or antelopes, there are trusts and charities set up to fund their survival. The extinction of a certain species would lead to widespread outrage.

The bottom line is that the extinction of any species would have far reaching effects. The natural ecosystem is a delicate chain, which has been crafted over hundreds of thousands of years of predator-prey relations. To throw a curveball such as extinction into the mix, would be devastating. Therefore, it is safe to say that the extinction of a species would matter a great deal.

Academic Reading: About the Test

IELTS Academic Reading

The IELTS Academic reading assessment is a comprehensive test of your reading ability. The test will last for 1 hour in total, and there will be 40 questions. The questions are designed to test elements such as:

- How well you can identify information after reading a text.

- How well you can understand writer's views and opinions.

- How efficiently you can 'skim read'.

- How well you can understand logic and arguments for/against the text.

- How much detail you can remember, having a read a text.

The test itself will encompass three long texts. The texts will vary. So, you might get one text which is particularly descriptive, one text which is factually based, and one text which is analytical. All of the texts will be taken from either a book, a journal, a magazine, or a newspaper. The texts have been deliberately chosen to be appropriate for people applying for a university course or wanting professional registration.

There are a huge variety of question types that you could see in the reading exam. Below we have provided you with a list of these, and what they involve. In our practice test, we've done our best to incorporate as many of these as possible, to give you lots of practice.

Question Type 1

In question type 1, candidates must choose the best answer from 4 options, or the best 2 answers from 5 options, or the best 3 answers from 7 options. All you need to do is write the letter of the correct answer on the answer sheet. In terms of the questions themselves, these will usually involve completing a sentence, filling in missing words, or just completing questions based on the text.

The questions here will usually be listed in the same order that they appear within the text.

For example, you might be asked:

Which of the following most accurately reflects the view of the author?

A – The author believes that animals are more important than humans

B – The author believes that humans are more important than animals.

C – The author believes that neither humans nor animals are important.

D – The author believes that humans and animals are equally important.

You then just need to read the text and select the best answer.

Question Type 2

In question type 2, candidates will be given a number of statements, and then will be asked to decide whether the statements are true, false, or not given, based on the information in the text. When answering these questions, you must use ONLY the information from the passage, and not any external knowledge from outside the text.

In our sample tests, 'not given' is listed as Impossible To Say.

For example, you might be asked:

Sort the following statements into the categories TRUE, FALSE or NOT GIVEN.

Q1. The author does not believe in animal rights.

Q2. The author does not believe in human rights.

Q3. There are seven yellow daisies in the garden.

Q4. Mary hates satsumas.

Question Type 3

In question type 3, candidates will be given a number of statements, and then will be asked to decide whether the statements agree with the views of the writer. Candidates will have to answer 'yes', 'no' or 'not given'.

For example, you might be asked:

Look at the following statements and decide whether the statement corresponds with the view of the writer. You must answer with yes, no, or not given.

1. We should launch a nuclear attack on Pluto.

2. The moon landings were faked.

3. Humans should continue with space exploration

4. Aliens do not exist.

Question Type 4

In question type 4, candidates will be asked to find specific information within lettered parts of the text, and then asked to identify which parts of information go with which bits. These could include finding certain details, lines of reasoning, descriptions, comparisons or points of view.

For example, you might be asked:

Match the following information up with the paragraph in which it appears. Label each line with the paragraph number in which it appears.

1. Two hundred people lost their lives today.

2. The blame for the incident fell on Commissioner Warren.

3. Mary was devastated by the loss of her husband.

4. The plague swept across the nation.

Question Type 5

In question type 5, candidates will be given a list of headings, which refer to ideas contained in the paragraphs. Candidates must then match the headings to the paragraphs or sections within the test.

For example, you might be asked:

Match the following headings to the ideas contained within specific paragraphs. Label each heading with the paragraph number that it matches up to.

1. Choices Have Consequences.

2. Pride Comes Before the Fall.

3. The Downfall of Man.

4. Journey's End.

Question Type 6

In question type 6, candidates will be given a set of statements/information, which they must then match up to lettered paragraphs within the text. You might be asked to match different qualities to certain categories of people, or events to time periods.

For example, you might be asked:

Match the following statements with the relevant paragraph.

1. Children of age five are likely to enjoy school the most.

2. Children between the ages of 6 and 8 are most likely to hate their parents.

3. Children attending primary school are likely to experience bullying.

4. Children entering their teenage years are more likely to argue with their parents.

Question Type 7

In question type 7, candidates will be given the first half of a sentence, and then asked to complete the sentence based on the text. Candidates will be given a number of answer options, and there will be more options than there are questions.

For example, you might be asked:

The author believes that there are too many, ...

A – variables to consider, before coming to a definitive conclusion.

B – inconsistencies in the information, meaning that reaching a conclusion is impossible.

C – people giving their opinion, all of whom need to mind their own business.

D – red flowers in his front garden.

E – spices in his wife's pasta dish.

Question Type 8

In question type 8, candidates must complete sentences using a specific number of words. The sentences will be based upon the text. The test will make it clear how many words should be used to complete the sentence, and candidates will lose marks for using more words than specified.

For example, you might be asked:

Complete the following sentences, using the text. You must give ONE word responses.

A – There are three yellow lemons in the fruit ....

B – Eight of the boys were diagnosed with.....

C – Green vegetables are the order of the ......

D – I received a low score in my ......

Question Type 9

In question type 9, test takers will be given a summary of a section of the text, and then will be asked to complete it using information that they've read in the text. For example, you might be given a table that is half completed, containing missing information, and your task is then to complete it using the text.

For example, you might be asked:

Fill in the table below, using information from the text. The first parts are done for you:

STUDENT TIMETABLES							
MARY	08:15		11:30		13:00	14:00	
	09:00		12:00	13:00	14:00	14:30	
BELINDA	08:00	09:00			14:00		

Question Type 10

In question type 10, candidates are asked to complete labels on a diagram. The diagram will relate to descriptions taken from the text. There will be a specific number of words allocated per answer, which will be made clear on the question sheet. If test takers write anything over the allocated number of words, then they will lose marks.

For example, you might be asked:

Complete the labels on the diagram below, using the text as a guide. You should write a maximum of two words for each label.

Question Type 11

In question type 11, you will be given a series of factually based questions, relating to information within the text. You will again be given a set number of words in which to answer.

For example, you might be asked:

Answer the following questions based on the text, using three words or less.

1. What is the name of the French woman, whom Sophie meets?

2. Why is Sophie going to the party, instead of her meeting?

3. How many people attended the party?

4. What was the cause of Samantha's death?

In our practice test, we have done our best to provide you with a wide variety of these questions. The actual test won't require you to answer every single type of question, instead you'll see a mixture of three or four, but it's random as to which one can come up. Our practice questions contain slight variations on all of these exercises, so they aren't exactly the same, but will test you in the same way and on the exact same skills.

Academic Reading: Practice Questions

Diving In Football

Speaker A – The popularity of modern football has reached an all-time high. Football is by far and away the most popular sport in the world. In a way, you could argue football has transcended sport itself. It has become a language, a means to bridge the gap between different kinds of people. Unless, of course, you are American. Unfortunately, as its popularity grows, so does the desperation to win. Now more than ever, the financial rewards for winning in football have grown disproportionate, and this has given rise to a new form of sporting cancer – diving.

Diving (or flopping as it's known in the USA) is the practice of faking or exaggerating injury, in order to con or cheat the referee – thereby gaining an advantage. Whether that advantage is a free kick or a penalty, the result is irrelevant. The bottom line is that this has to stop. The phrase 'football is a man's game' is horrendously outdated, but there is some truth behind it.

Not only is diving cheating, but it slows the game down. It's embarrassing to watch perfectly healthy athletes pretending to be hurt, and it's even worse when your team suffers the consequences of it. Cheating is cheating, plain and simple. We need to kick this out of the game, before it kills football altogether.

Speaker B – One of the biggest debates currently raging in football at the moment, particularly in the United Kingdom, is on the issue of diving. Speak to almost any football fan in the UK about the subject of diving, and you'll be met with anger, rage and frustration. You'll hear silly phrases such as 'football is a man's game' and 'diving is cheating'. Britain's rage towards diving is palpable. More so than any other country, Britain holds the moral integrity of its footballers above all else. The ideal British footballer is strong, quick and above all else – honest. The problem with this image is that it's just not true.

In reality, Britain has become absurdly hypocritical with its footballers. Diving is seen as one of the ultimate evils, yet crunching leg breaking tackles are openly cheered. A bevy of footballers have lined up to admit that they openly set out to hurt the opposition, and certain managers rejoice in inflicting physical pain on the opposition. Yet in Britain, these people are not villains. Some of them are even seen as heroes. What is worse, openly jeopardising the career of a fellow professional, or seeking to gain an unfair advantage? Life is about taking advantage of your opportunities.

In football, just as in any other area of life, there will be people who cheat to get ahead. I am not suggesting we should let this go unpunished, but it is what it is. Let's not kid ourselves – diving IS cheating. However, it's nowhere near as bad as British football would have you believe, and it certainly doesn't put other players at risk.

Answer the following questions based on the information from the passage.

Q1. Speaker A starts off his argument by discussing the popularity of football. What is the most likely reason that he does this?

A – To show that as football becomes more popular, people are becoming more desperate to win.

B – To show that football has become morally bankrupt.

C – To show that football risks losing its popularity.

D – To show that he does not like football.

Q2. In paragraph 2, speaker A uses the term 'bottom line'. What is the name for this type of phrase?

A – Idiomatic

B – Platonic

C – Idiosyncratic

D – Nomothetic

Q3. What is the overall point that Speaker A is trying to make?

A – Diving is not manly.

B – Diving is embarrassing.

C – Diving is outdated

D – Diving needs to be stopped

Q4. Which of the following is implied by Speaker B?

A – Britain has a hypocritical attitude towards diving.

B – Diving needs to be banned.

C – UK football fans are angry and frustrated.

D – Diving is more acceptable than setting out to hurt the opposition.

Q5. Speaker B believes which of the following to be true?

A – Britain needs to accept that cheating is acceptable.

B – That speaker A is hypocritical and deluded.

C – Britain holds its footballers to a higher moral standard than other parts of the world.

D – British football will ultimately suffer the competitive consequences of their failure to embrace diving, as they will be outwitted and beaten by smarter opponents.

Q6. Speaker B says that 'life is about taking advantage of your opportunities.' What does he mean by this?

A – That if you don't make the most of your life, you will always have regrets.

B – That you only get one chance at life, so you need to make the most of it.

C – That if footballers see an opportunity to fool the referees, they should take it.

D – That footballers have a unique opportunity, and are wasting it by trying to con referees.

Q7. Speaker A and B differ on which of the following views?

A – Speaker A believes that diving, in the long-term, will see the end of football. Speaker B believes that although diving is overestimated, it could be responsible for the downfall of the sport of football.

B – Speaker A believes that diving, if not punished, could kill football as a sport altogether. Speaker B thinks that Britain grossly exaggerates how bad diving is.

C – Speaker A feels that diving is a cancer that needs to be eliminated from the sport altogether. Speaker B compares diving to 'stealing pennies from the kitchen counter.'

D – Speaker A feels that players who dive should be banned for life. Speaker B believes that diving is a skill which should be rewarded.

Now look at the following statements, and work out whether they correspond with the information given in the passage. Your answer options are as follows:

TRUE. You should only select this if the statement can be verified by the passage.

FALSE. You should only select this if the statement contradicts the information in the passage.

IMPOSSIBLE TO SAY. You should only select this if the passage does not give enough information on the statement for it to be verified as true or false.

Q8. Diving is the practice of feigning injury, to try and fool spectators.

TRUE	FALSE	IMPOSSIBLE TO SAY

Q9. Both Speaker A and B agree that diving is cheating.

TRUE	FALSE	IMPOSSIBLE TO SAY

Q10. In the USA, diving is known as flopping.

TRUE	FALSE	IMPOSSIBLE TO SAY

Q11. Speaker A thinks that South American footballers are the worst cheaters.

TRUE	FALSE	IMPOSSIBLE TO SAY

Q12. Speaker B strongly implies that diving is a lesser crime than bad tackling.

TRUE	FALSE	IMPOSSIBLE TO SAY

Q13. Speaker A believes that the monetary prizes given to winning football teams are too low.

TRUE	FALSE	IMPOSSIBLE TO SAY

Q14. Both Speaker A and Speaker B hold the phrase 'football is a man's game' in contempt.

TRUE	FALSE	IMPOSSIBLE TO SAY

Q15. Speaker B believes that football could benefit from taking the same approach to cheating as tennis.

TRUE	FALSE	IMPOSSIBLE TO SAY

Can Creative Writing Be Taught?

One of the mostly hotly debated topics in academic circles is on the subject of creative writing. Amongst academics and humanities students, you'll often find that there is a clear split in opinion on the validity of creative writing as a taught subject.

Naysayers' first port of call when it comes to a debate on the subject, is to claim that writing is not something that can be delivered in lesson format. They believe creative writing is an exercise in itself. That is to say, your writing will only improve as you improve your relationship with language, speech and words, and even then, it's not enough. The most beautiful prose is entirely inadequate without a good story behind it; and you can't teach someone how to write a good story. You can show them structure and narrative form, and direct their attention to other fantastic authors, but ultimately a great story has to come from within you. It's your story, and only you can tell it.

Other non-believers claim that the problem isn't with the subject itself, it's with the way that lecturers are naturally inclined to teach it. Creative writing lessons, they say, simply become a way for lecturers to turn students into a pastiche of themselves, with little to no direction of their own. We all have our own style of writing, that we also enjoy reading. When giving advice or critiquing other writer's work, we naturally lean towards an opinion that corresponds with our own. That is to say, we advise them to write what we like to read, which is naturally the same as the way we like to write.

This is dangerous when it comes to new and aspiring writers, who are still searching for a way to define their own style. Through workshop feedback, student writers gradually turn into a poorer clone of their lecturers, and are then marked higher than other more unique students as a result. Critics claim that writing degrees are killing the creativity of the future generation, whilst taking bombastic fees for the trouble of doing so.

Then, there is the marking system itself. Along with the fact that the markers are naturally biased, questions have been asked over how it is that writing can be assigned a marked score. Can you really grade a piece of writing from 1-100? Written fiction is not the same as an essay, it is subjective, and to assign a score from 1-100 or even a grade (for example Pass, Merit, Distinction) seems utterly benign. The whole point of a creative writing degree is that you should improve as a writer, not what mark you get at the end of it. Unfortunately, biased marking, along with the credentials that arise from gaining a distinction, mean that some students naturally deviate from their normal work to produce prose that is more in line with what lecturers are looking for. That is to say, in order to achieve high marks, these students simply produce stylistically carbon copies of their lecturers own writing; rather than focusing on their own work. Monkey see, monkey do. Naturally those who don't conform then receive lower marks, while egotistical lecturers are more than happy to give out higher grades to those who attend their extra-curricular events, or meet up at the pub after classes.

Subjective marking means that shy or individualistic students are being punished, where students who wise up and smell the mustard are coming out of their writing degrees with better results; but no concept of how to write publishable material. The question is, which would you rather be?

Complete the questions below, based on the passage.

Q16. Select the words which best fit the gaps in this sentence

The author of this piece begins in a ……… fashion, citing various critical beliefs. However, the essay quickly descends into an ……….. piece, with the author clearly having strong ……. about the topic.

A – opinionated, orthodox, morals

B – unexpected, angry, reservations

C – philosophical, inspiring, persuasions

D – critical, persuasive, decisions

E – neutral, opinion, views

F – biased, uneducated, idiosyncrasies

G – unorthodox, irresistible, temptations

Q17. The author describes the fees for taught Creative Writing as 'bombastic'. In relation to the passage, which of the following is the most accurate definition of this?

A – The fees being charged for Creative Writing are disproportionate for the amount of work being put in by the student.

B – The fees being charged for Creative Writing are disproportionate to what students will actually get out of the experience.

C – The fees being charged for Creative Writing are disproportionate when taking into account that this should be a free service.

D – The fees being charged for Creative Writing are simply a way to line the teachers' pockets, so that they can get better publishing deals on their own work.

Q18. In relation to the passage, complete the missing word from this sentence.

The writer of this work believes that, as a consequence of biased marking, more and more students are turning to _____ of their lecturers' work.

A – Parodies

B – Criticising

C – Eulogising

D – Imitations

Q19. One of the biggest problems that the author has with taught creative writing, is the ………… lecturers.

Fill in the missing word, which best completes the sentence.

A – wealthy

B – fraudulent

C – egotistical

D – benign

Q20. The author believes that a writing degree should help students to accomplish which of the following:

A – Becoming an Amazon bestselling author.

B – Getting their book on advertisement signs and billboards.

C – Improving the quality of their writing.

D – Learning to write in the same way as their lecturers.

E – Socialising and getting to meet other writers at the local pub.

F – Achieving impressive grades.

```
┌─────────────────────────────────┐
│                                 │
│                                 │
└─────────────────────────────────┘
```

Q21. The author uses the phrase 'wise up and smell the mustard'. In the context of the passage, what does this phrase mean?

A – The author is saying that students who enjoy the taste of mustard are more likely to achieve a high mark, since Creative Writing lecturers are huge fans of the yellow condiment.

B – The author is saying that students who can demonstrate their ability to write in a wise and considered manner, are more likely to achieve high marks.

C – The author is saying that students who can behave in a calculated and underhanded fashion, stepping over those can't, will achieve the highest possible marks.

D – The author is saying that students who wise up to the way that biased marking works, are more likely to produce work which matches what the lecturers are looking for.

Q22. Which of the following words best summarises the tone of this work?

A – Exasperated

B – Hyperbolic

C – Incandescent

D – Aloof

E – Curious

Match the following information to a specific paragraph in the text. There are 6 paragraphs in total. Some of the information is paraphrased.

Q23. 'Writing fiction is not the same as an essay, it is subjective.'

Q24. 'When giving advice or critiquing other writer's work, we naturally lean towards an opinion that corresponds with our own.'

Q25. 'Grading a piece of writing from 1-100 seems benign'.

Q26. 'Even the most beautifully written prose will not make up for a badly written story'.

Complete the following sentence in accordance with the writer's viewpoint:

Q27. The writer of this piece strongly believes that……

A – Creative writing is a multi-faceted, complicated subject, which makes any debate over the teaching of this subject pointless.

B – Creative writing lecturers are using their students as way of fuelling their own delusional fantasies, of grandeur and pomposity.

C – Creative writing is an individual exercise, which examines the writer's sense of 'self'.

D – Creative writing cannot be judged or marked, because it is simply too subjective.

E – Creative writing students should make a concerted attempt to visit the pubs with their lecturers, because then they will receive higher marks.

Q28. Which of the following is in contradiction with the writer's view about the principle aim of a writing degree?

A – A creative writing degree should be used to demonstrate to employers that a writer's work is of a high standard.

B – A creative writing degree cannot be seen as an indication that a writer has talent or skill.

C – A creative writing degree mark should be used as an indication of whether someone is a good or bad writer.

D – Your success on a writing degree ultimately comes down to how many of the lecturers you can befriend.

E – Creative writing degrees are largely scorned by the majority of employers.

Q29. Complete the following sentence in accordance with the passage:

Students who copy their lecturers' style will ultimately…

A – produce a poorer quality piece of work, than those written by their lecturers.

B – produce better quality work than their lecturers.

C – learn the ins and outs of their lecturers' style, ultimately bettering their teachers.

D – receive lower marks, as lecturers don't like copycats.

E – fail to improve their own writing, and receive lower marks as a result.

Q30. The writer believes which of the following to be true?

A – That the academic community is largely split on the validity of creative writing as a taught subject.

B – That the academic community is widely unified against the teaching of creative writing.

C – That creative writing has been largely accepted as a taught subject by the academic community.

D – That creative writing will never be accepted by the academic community, because it's so subjective.

E – That creative writing as a taught subject is utterly irrelevant, and garners no respect in the academic community.

Stalin vs Trotsky

In the wake of Lenin's death, a power struggle emerged within the Bolshevik party of the Soviet Union. On the one side, was Joseph Stalin. Cold, mechanical and more ruthless than anyone could have imagined, Lenin's deathbed testament warned the other members of the Politburo against the General Secretary. On the other side, Leon Trotsky. Arrogant, brash but infinitely more idealistic than Stalin, the general expectation was that Trotsky would be the natural successor to Lenin. As it happened, Stalin astutely outmanoeuvred Trotsky, and the latter was exiled from the country.

On the face of it, it is quite shocking that Trotsky failed. Here was an astute, Jewish politician (widely regarded as far more intelligent than Stalin) who had been personally recommended by Lenin's testament; theoretically Trotsky should have naturally stepped into the space left by the former.

There are several reasons why this did not happen. Firstly, the testament of Lenin was hidden by Stalin and other members of the party. The letter (although excusing them) drew attention to Kamenev and Zinoviev's doubts over the 1917 revolution, and thus it was beneficial for them to aid Stalin in covering this up. Together, the three formed a 'troika' against Trotsky – who inexplicably chose to remain on holiday after Lenin died, and failed to make any kind of public eulogy. This was compounded by Trotsky's notoriously prickly and over-confident nature, which riled the other members of the Politburo. Indeed it was perhaps this over-confidence which led Trotsky to underestimate Stalin, and fall for extremely basic deception – such as being given the wrong date for Lenin's funeral.

More importantly, Trotsky's own ideology posed another problem. An idealist, Trotsky wanted to expand the socialist revolution throughout the world, and cause an international uprising. Stalin's ideas were centralised at home; he believed that concentrated socialism in the anti-Semitic USSR would make Mother Russia stronger in the long run. Stalin used Trotsky's ideas against him, claiming that they were a threat to the nation.

Ultimately, Stalin capitalised where Trotsky could not. He recognised an opportunity to consolidate power, using the name of Lenin to back himself, and carried this out with ruthless effectiveness. By 1940, Trotsky was dead – exiled and assassinated at Stalin's command. So too were Kamenev, Zinoviev, Bukharin and Rykov. With nobody left to oppose him, Uncle Joe had won.

Q31. Which of the following is NOT given as a reason for Trotsky's failure?

A – Trotsky severely underestimated Stalin, due to his own overconfidence.

B – Trotsky was Jewish, in an anti-semitic country.

C – Stalin lied to Trotsky, and gave him the wrong date for Lenin's funeral.

D – Trotsky's foreign policy.

Q32. Which of the following best summarises the author's views towards Trotsky?

A – Trotsky was a highly capable and intelligent politician, who severely underestimated his opponent.

B – Trotsky was an arrogant and overconfident fool, who turned everyone in the party against him.

C – Trotsky was the victim of a Politburo-wide conspiracy, and was forced out of the party by underhanded tactics.

D – Trotsky failed to recognise the needs of the Russian people, and therefore was ousted from his seat in government.

Q33. What does the author imply about Lenin's testament?

A – Lenin's testament would have been the difference between Stalin and Trotsky taking power.

B – Lenin's testament would have significantly increased Trotsky's chances of taking power.

C – Lenin's testament was inaccurate and would not have made a difference to who took power.

D – Lenin's testament was hidden by Stalin, Kamenev and Zinoviev; in order to make sure nobody read his criticism of them.

Q34. In paragraph 2, the author states, 'On the face of it, it is quite shocking that Trotsky failed.' What does she mean by this?

A – It seems surprising to the author that Trotsky failed, and she is still trying to come to terms with why this was.

B – It seems surprising that Trotsky failed, until you look at his obvious political shortcomings.

C – It seems surprising that Trotsky failed, until you look at the level of opposition that he was up against.

D – It seems surprising that Trotsky failed, if you look at the position he was in when Lenin died.

Q35. On the basis of this passage, which of the following is it safe to assume?

A – Kamenev and Zinoviev's alliance with Stalin did not last.

B – Kamenev and Zinoviev were complicit in the execution of Bukharin.

C – Kamenev and Zinoviev allied with Stalin against Rykov.

D – Stalin used Kamenev and Zinoviev's doubts about the 1917 revolution against them.

Q36. Based on the passage, which of the following best describes the difference between Trotsky and Stalin's view?

A – Stalin wanted to unite the people of Russia behind a common cause, before launching all-out war on the West. Trotsky wanted to go to war immediately.

B – Stalin saw that Russia needed to build from within, if it was to become a world power. Trotsky wanted Russia to run before it could walk.

C – Stalin wanted Russia to build its strength internally. Trotsky wanted to spread communism throughout the world.

D – Stalin felt that Russia would be better off focusing on matters at home. Trotsky wanted to go to war with Britain.

[   ]

In the following questions, match the idea presented with the paragraph in which it appears.

Q37. The majority of people expected that Trotsky would be the successor to Lenin.

[   ]

Q38. Trotsky did not make any public statement following Lenin's death, expressing his sorrow.

[   ]

Q39. Stalin systematically eliminated every single person who might have opposed him.

[   ]

Q40. Trotsky was considered arrogant by the other members of the party.

[   ]

Academic Reading:
Answers

Q1. *Answer = A. To show that as football becomes more popular, people are becoming more desperate to win.*

Explanation = The author frames his argument by suggesting that there is a relationship between the rising popularity of football, and the desperation to win. Later in the first paragraph, the author directly states, 'Unfortunately, as its popularity grows, so does the desperation to win.'

Q2. *Answer = A. Idiomatic.*

Explanation = An idiomatic phrase is an informal English expression, containing words which mean different to what is used in the expression. For example, 'bottom line' does not mean the bottom/lowest/very last line; it means 'the definitive truth'.

Q3. *Answer = D. Diving needs to be stopped.*

Explanation = Speaker A is clearly trying to show that diving needs to be stopped. While he does describe diving as embarrassing and not manly, these are both just used to illustrate a wider argument. Similarly, the term outdated is used to describe the term 'football is a man's game', not diving itself.

Q4. *Answer = D. Diving is more acceptable than setting out to hurt the opposition.*

Explanation = The author does not directly state that diving is more acceptable than setting out to hurt the opposition, but it is strongly implied via his choice of words. For example, the author asks the rhetorical question, 'What is worse, openly jeopardising the career of a fellow professional, or seeking to gain an unfair advantage?' He does this to make a point, without directly stating it.

Q5. *Answer = C. Britain holds its footballers to a higher moral standard than other parts of the world.*

Explanation = Speaker B clearly states that 'more so than any other country, Britain holds the moral integrity of its footballers above all else. The ideal British footballer is strong, quick and above all else – honest.' In other words, Britain holds its footballers to a higher moral standard.

Q6. *Answer = C. That if footballers see an opportunity to fool the referees, they should take it.*

Explanation = In the context of the passage, this is the only answer that makes sense.

Q7. Answer = B. Speaker A believes that diving, if not punished, could kill football as a sport altogether. Speaker B thinks that Britain grossly exaggerates how bad diving is.

Explanation = When looking at the passage, we can see the following quotes: Speaker A says, 'Cheating is cheating, plain and simple. We need to kick this out of the game, before it kills football altogether.' Speaker B says, 'Let's not kid ourselves – diving IS cheating. However, it's nowhere near as bad as British football would have you believe.'

Q8. False

Q9. True

Q10. True

Q11. Impossible to Say

Q12. True

Q13. False

Q14. True

Q15. Impossible to Say

Q16. *Answer = E. neutral, opinion, views*

Explanation = The author of this piece begins in a neutral fashion, citing various critical beliefs. However, the essay quickly descends into an opinion piece, with the author clearly having strong views about the topic.

Q17. *Answer = B. The fees being charged for Creative Writing are disproportionate to what students will actually get out of the experience.*

Explanation = Prior to this sentence, the author claims that Creative Writing degrees are killing students' creativity. Furthermore, the author later says that the whole point of a Creative Writing degree is for students to improve their writing style and quality of work. Therefore, if we assume that Creative Writing degrees are doing the opposite of this, then students are being overcharged for what they will get from the experience.

Q18. *Answer = D. Imitations.*

Explanation = The author clearly states, 'Creative writing lessons, they say, simply become a way for lecturers to turn students into a pastiche of themselves, with little to no direction of their own.' The word pastiche indicates that students are producing imitations of their lecturers' work.

Q19. *Answer = C. Egotistical.*

Explanation = The writer states, '…while egotistical lecturers are more than happy to give out higher grades to those who attend their extra-curricular events, or meet up at the pub after classes.'

Q20. *Answer = C. Improving the quality of their writing.*

Explanation = The writer states, 'The whole point of a creative writing degree is that you should improve as a writer, not what mark you get at the end of it.'

Q21. *Answer = D. The author is saying that students who wise up to the way that biased marking works, are more likely to produce work which matches what the lecturers are looking for.*

Explanation = In relation to the passage, this is the answer that makes the most sense. The author states, '…students who wise up and smell the mustard are coming out of their writing degrees with better results.' Therefore, there is a clear link between the phrase and the mark itself.

Q22. *Answer = A. Exasperated.*

Explanation = The term 'exasperated' essentially means being irritated and frustrated. This is the most accurate definition of the author's mood, as they are clearly frustrated by the way Creative Writing degrees are being run.

Q23. Paragraph 5

Q24. Paragraph 3

Q25. Paragraph 5

Q26. Paragraph 2

Q27. *Answer = D. Creative writing cannot be judged or marked, because it is simply too subjective.*

Explanation = Of all the sentences, this is the most accurate. The writer definitively states, 'Can you really grade a piece of writing from 1-100? Written fiction is not the same as an essay, it is subjective, and to assign a score from 1-100 or even a grade (for example Pass, Merit, Distinction) seems utterly benign.'

Q28. *Answer = D. Your success on a writing degree ultimately comes down to how many of the lecturers you can befriend.*

Explanation = The writer's main view of Creative Writing degrees is that they should be used to improve the quality of participants' writing. Therefore, if a person has improved the quality of their writing, they can consider this a success. Option D contradicts this, insinuating that if you haven't befriended the lecturers, then you can't consider it a success.

Q29. *Answer = A. produce a poorer quality piece of work, than those written by their lecturers.*

Explanation = The author clearly states that, 'student writers gradually turn into a poorer clone of their lecturers, and are then marked higher than other more unique students as a result.'

Q30. *Answer = A. That the academic community is largely split on the validity of creative writing as a taught subject.*

Explanation = The author clearly states, 'Amongst academics and humanities students, you'll often find that there is a clear split in opinion on the validity of creative writing as a taught subject.'

Q31. *Answer = B. Trotsky was Jewish, in an anti-semitic country.*

Explanation = The passage mentions that Trotsky was Jewish, but does not cast this in a negative light or accuse Russia of anti-semitism.

Q32. *Answer = A. Trotsky was a highly capable and intelligent politician, who severely underestimated his opponent.*

Explanation = Answer A is the most accurate. The author is happy to give credit to Trotsky, referring to him as 'astute' and 'intelligent' but also recognises that Trotsky underestimated Stalin, and made mistakes, 'inexplicably chose to remain on holiday'.

Q33. *Answer = B. Lenin's testament would have significantly increased Trotsky's chances of taking power.*

Explanation = While Answer D is correct, the author directly states this. It is not implied. The author does not however directly state that Lenin's testament would have aided Trotsky. She simply refers to the fact that Lenin's testament recommended Trotsky, and this is one of the reasons it was hidden (along with criticising Stalin, Kamenev and Zinoviev).

Q34. *Answer = D. It seems surprising that Trotsky failed, if you look at the position he was in when Lenin died.*

Explanation = The author uses the phrase 'on the face of it' to show that looking at the strength of Trotsky's position when Lenin died, it is quite shocking that he failed. She follows this up by stating why Trotsky's position was so strong.

Q35. Answer = A. Kamenev and Zinoviev's alliance with Stalin did not last.

Explanation = At the end of this passage, the author states, 'By 1940, Trotsky was dead – exiled and assassinated at Stalin's command. So too were Kamenev, Zinoviev, Bukharin and Rykov.'

Q36. Answer = C. Stalin wanted Russia to build its strength internally. Trotsky wanted to spread communism throughout the world.

Explanation = The author states, 'Trotsky wanted to expand the socialist revolution throughout the world, and cause an international uprising. Stalin's ideas were centralised at home; he believed that concentrated socialism in the anti-Semitic USSR would make Mother Russia stronger in the long run.' Therefore, C is the most accurate.

Q37. Paragraph 1

Q38. Paragraph 3

Q39. Paragraph 5

Q40. Paragraph 3

General Training Writing: About the Test

IELTS General Training is designed for candidates migrating to the UK, Canada or Australia, or who are applying for secondary education or work experience/training in an environment where English is the primary language.

In this part of the book, we'll give you a full breakdown of both the General Training writing and reading exercises.

Let's start with the writing test.

IELTS General Training: Writing

The IELTS General Training exercise is a test designed to focus on your ability to demonstrate the following qualities:

- A strong level of vocabulary.

- An ability to think creatively, demonstrating your ability to improvise, using words.

- A strong level of grammar and accuracy.

- Using description and instruction, along with persuasive language.

- Your ability to argue in a coherent and logical fashion.

- Your ability to tailor written communication to suitable readers and audiences.

There are two tasks in the IELTS General Training Writing, and these are as follows:

Task 1
In Task 1, you will be given a specific situation, and will then be asked to write a response to this, in 150 words or more. Your response will be in the form of a letter, which can be either formal or informal depending on the subject, and will generally be written in response to an everyday, common situation – for example, making a complaint to someone, or writing a letter to your landlord.

Here's a classic example of how a question of this type might look:

You are the leader of a team in your workplace. Your team has been tasked with showing prospective investors why they should invest in your company. Your head of department has asked you to write the investors a short letter, explaining the benefits of investing. In your letter, you must explain:

- *What bonuses the company can offer investors.*

- *What the financial rewards of investing with your company would be.*

- *Your company's ethos and philosophy.*

Your answer should be 150 words or more. It should start with the words, 'Dear Mrs Marsham…'

After each question, you will be given 3 bullet points which explain the type of information that must be included in the response. For example, you might be told, 'you must include the time of the meeting in your response.'

Part of the skill of this exercise involves identifying what tone to take in your letter. You need to establish what the correct approach is, either formal or informal, and then write in a style which is appropriate for the audience. For example, if you were writing to your boss then you would take a formal approach. If you were writing to a close friend, you will take an informal approach.

Whilst writing, it's important that you don't deviate. You must stick to the topic and ensure that you include the information from the bullet points. However, there is room for some creativity. The question won't have every single bit of information that needs to go in the letter – some of this you will have to make up.

You have 20 minutes to construct your response to this question.

As in the IELTS Academic, Task 1 is worth half as much as Task 2.

Task 2

Task 2 is highly similar to task 2 of the Academic Writing, where you will be asked to write a discursive essay, of 250 words or more. The question will give you a point of view, subject, or argument, and then ask you to discuss this. The topics are of general interest; For example, they may discuss subjects like whether Britain should have a monarchy, the logic behind patriotism, environmental problems, smoking in public places, etc.

For example, you might be asked:

'Many people believe that social media is having a dangerous and

negative impact on human interactions, and is harmful for our long term future.

In 250 words or more, discuss your views on this.'

In your response, you need to argue for/against a particular view. Although it's always good if you can acknowledge counter arguments, you have 40 minutes and 250 words to do this, so usually it's better to focus on one side of the argument, whilst trying to be as persuasive, logical and fluent as possible. Your writing quality and your vocabulary are being assessed in this exercise, so it's important that you can put together a coherent and logical response, paying attention to grammar, spelling and punctuation, whilst addressing the main statement from the question.

Now, have a go at our practice questions!

General Training Writing: Practice Questions

TASK 1

Q1. You are a teacher at a school, and you have recently discovered that one of your pupils, Violet, is being bullied by two other students. The names of the bullies are Phoebe and Susie. Your head of department has asked for you to write her a letter, explaining what you are intending to do about the situation. In your letter, you must explain:

- The things that Phoebe and Susie have been doing/saying to Violet.

- How this has impacted Violet.

- What you intend to do about the situation.

Your answer should be 150 words or more. It should start with the words, 'Dear Mrs Winchester…'

Q2. Your partner is going shopping today to buy ingredients for some recipes that you are cooking tonight. He will also need to pick up party supplies: including birthday hats, ribbons and a cake. The recipe is for a large pasta dish, consisting of chicken and peas. The pasta must be brown. In your letter, you must explain:

- Which supermarket your partner needs to visit.

- Which ingredients he needs to pick up for the pasta dish.

- The names of any party supplies.

Your answer should be 150 words or more. It should start with the words, 'Dear Paul...'

Q3. You are working for the UK Police. Your Detective Inspector has asked you to write up a short report, explaining an incident that occurred last Tuesday. On the date in question, you and your colleague were forced to intervene in a situation, and arrest a 16-year-old boy, named Benjamin, for assault. In your letter, you must explain:

- Why you arrested the boy.

- What occurred during the situation.

- Whether you and your colleague could have done anything better.

Your answer should be 150 words or more. It should start with the words, 'Dear Inspector Bryant…'

Q4. Your pet cat, Pickles, is being placed into a cattery (hotel for cats) whilst you go on a business trip. The trip will last for 2 weeks. Your task is to write a letter to the owner of the cattery, explaining:

- Any dietary requirements that are needed for Pickles.

- Any specific behavioural characteristics which the cattery should know about.

- What time Pickles likes to wake up and go to bed.

Your answer should be 150 words or more. It should start with the words, 'Dear Wendy…'

Q5. One of your friends recently moved to America. You have not seen him for 3 months, but you have tried to stay in contact via letters and emails. He recently wrote you a letter, and now you need to respond. In your letter, you should explain:

- What your current work situation is, and whether you enjoy your job.

- How your health is, and whether you are taking any steps to improve it.

- How your family is.

Your answer should be 150 words or more. It should start with the words, 'Dear Frederick…'

Q6. You have decided that the time has come to resign from your company. Although you've been working there for 3 years, you have been unhappy with the progress of the company lately. Your task is to write a letter to your boss, telling him why you are resigning. In your letter, you should explain:

- The reasons for your resignation.

- Any plans for the future.

- Your thoughts on management and the company.

Your answer should be 150 words or more. It should start with the words, 'Dear Mr Fudley…'

Q7. You are writing to the manager of a local restaurant, to complain about the treatment that you and your husband received whilst dining there. Both of you felt that the treatment from the staff and the service was appalling. In your letter, you should explain:

- What it was about the restaurant that was so bad.

- What you would like to be done about it.

- What happened during your visit to the restaurant.

Your answer should be 150 words or more. It should start with the words, 'Dear Mrs Wibbley…'

Q8. You are working as a teacher. Your task is to write a letter to a parent, about the behaviour of their son, Kevin, during your classes. The boy in question has been behaving extremely poorly, and you have decided that now is the time to deal with this behaviour. Your letter should request to meet with the parent. In your letter, you should explain:

- How the pupil has been behaving, and why this is disruptive.

- What you think should be done about it.

- When you are available to meet with the parent.

Your answer should be 150 words or more. It should start with the words, 'Dear Mr Gildsworth...'

Q9. You are writing to your landlord, to express concerns over the flat that you are staying in. The purpose of your letter is to ask the landlord to fix various issues, and explain why these issues are detrimental to your standard of living. In your letter, you should explain:

- What exactly the issues are with your flat, and why they are causing problems.

- When it would be suitable for the landlord to visit you.

- Whether you are at fault for any of the issues.

Your answer should be 150 words or more. It should start with the words, 'Dear Paul…'

Q10. You have recently been placed in charge of a work team. Unfortunately, the team doesn't seem to be responding particularly well to your management. As a result, you are writing to your boss for some advice. In your letter, you should explain:

- What the problems are.

- Why you think the problems are occurring.

- What you have tried to do to fix them.

Your answer should be 150 words or more. It should start with the words, 'Dear Mrs Everett…'

Q11. You are writing to the head of a train company – Ficshire Rail – to complain about the services this morning. You were delayed by 30 minutes this morning, and as a result missed an important work meeting. Your letter must make it clear how unhappy you are with Ficshire Rail. In your letter you should explain:

- Why you think the fees are extortionate.

- Your concerns about train delay times.

- What you think should be done about it.

Your answer should be 150 words or more. It should start with the words, 'Dear Mr Steel…'

Q12. You have missed the deadline for your university essay, and now you need to explain to your professor why this was the case. The essay was weighted at 50% of your final grade. In your letter, you should explain:

- Why you missed the deadline.

- When you will be able to submit the final piece of work.

- How you intend to improve your performance in future.

Your answer should be 150 words or more. It should start with the words, 'Dear Professor Minchin…'

Q13. You work for a data collection agency. Unfortunately, this week, disaster has struck – and there has been an enormous information leak, of an unprecedented scale. Nobody knows who is responsible. You need to write a letter to your boss, telling her what you are doing to resolve the situation. In your letter, you should explain:

- Where the data leak originated from, and what you are doing to find out who is responsible.

- What steps you are taking to resolve the situation.

- How you will prevent such things from happening in future.

Your answer should be 150 words or more. It should start with the words, 'Dear Mrs Perkins…'

Q14. Your partner has asked you to write a letter to a close friend, thanking them for inviting the pair of you to their wedding. In your letter, you should explain:

- What you enjoyed the most about the wedding.

- Any things you didn't like about the wedding.

- Whether you'd like to see your friend in the near future.

Your answer should be 150 words or more. It should start with the words, 'Dear Becky…'

Q15. You are organising a company event. Your responsibility is to communicate with the owner of a potential venue about what requirements the event needs, to establish whether the venue can meet these. In your letter, you should explain:

- How many people the event will be catering for.

- What type of facilities the venue must have.

- The overall budget for the venue, that the company are willing to pay.

Your answer should be 150 words or more. It should start with the words, 'Dear Patrick...'

TASK 2

Q16. *'In British schools, PE is compulsory. Students are required to take part in physical exercise lessons, to stay fit and healthy.'*

Do you think it's fair for schools to force students to exercise? Discuss your views on this topic in 250 words or more.

Q17. *'Gun control is one of the most popular topics of debate in the USA.'*

Discuss your views on whether you think people should be able to carry a weapon in public, and gun control in general, in 250 words or more.

Q18. *'Ethical veganism is a viewpoint which applies to those who follow a vegan diet for ethical reasons – such as the protection of animals, whilst also being against the use of animals for purposes such as work.'*

Discuss your views on ethical veganism, in 250 words or more.

Q19. *'Patriotism is a complex subject. It can just as easily lead to conflict as it can to unity and love.'*

Discuss your views on patriotism, in 250 words or more.

Q20. *'Over the past ten years, social networking has become a fundamental part of our lives. Still though, questions remain about the dangers of social networking, and the impact that it has on our lives.'*

Discuss your thoughts about social media, in 250 words or more.

Q21. The term 'fake news' is a commonly used term in today's society.

Explain what you think this term means, and discuss your views on whether you believe it is harmful, in 250 words or more.

Q22. *'One of the most interesting moral debates, is about whether human beings have a moral obligation towards people whom they've never met before. Should we care about someone we've never met, and probably never will meet?'*

Discuss your views on this subject, in 250 words or more.

Q23. *'Naturally, the term 'war' has very negative connotations. However, is it possible that there are some benefits to war? Has war had any positive impact on the human race?'*

Discuss your views on this, in 250 words or more.

Q24. *'Global warming is largely blamed on humans, but is this fair? Is it possible that natural processes are also, equally, to blame?'*

Discuss your views on this subject, in 250 words or more.

Q25. *'Can violence ever be justified? We are taught that violence is never the answer, but is this really the case?'*

Discuss your thoughts on this subject, in 250 words or more.

General Training Writing: Answers

Q1.

Answer

Dear Mrs Winchester,

I am writing to inform you about the situation surrounding one of our pupils, Violet. As you know, we have recently discovered that Violet has been the subject of bullying by another two pupils, Phoebe and Susie.

I first discovered that this was happening when Violet came to me for assistance. She claims that Phoebe and Susie have been kicking and punching her, usually after school hours, and that they have threatened her with further violence if she tells anyone. After some investigation and speaking to both Phoebe and Susie, I can verify that these allegations are true.

Violet has been deeply upset by this behaviour and informed me that she has been unable to sleep since it started – about two months ago.

In order to resolve this situation, I strongly suggest that both Phoebe and Susie are reprimanded (at the very least with a suspension) and that Violet is given significant support and counselling.

Yours sincerely,

Anne.

Q2.

Answer

Dear Paul,

As per our discussion earlier, I will need you go to visit Pembury Supermarket. The first thing we need is the ingredients for the pasta dish. With this in mind, I will require you to buy four packets of penne pasta. Please note that the pasta must be brown, not white. We will also need 5 roast chickens, and 6 bags of peas. Please could you also pick up some spices for the dish whilst you are at it – coriander and parsley would be great.

We will also need some party supplies. So, please make sure you purchase a selection of party hats – purple with ribbons and glitter on them, plastic cups, plastic plates and 6 boxes of napkins. We'll need a large sparkly Happy Birthday banner, and if the supermarket sells balloons then please pick these up too. I'm confident that you can find some balloons in the utility section of the supermarket.

See you later,

Jenny.

Q3.

Answer

Dear Inspector Bryant,

As requested, I am writing to inform you about the incident that occurred last Tuesday. On the day in question, myself and my colleague were on patrol on North Ficshire high street. Our attention was drawn to an incident 200 yards away, where two boys were apparently rolling around on the floor. We quickly approached the two individuals, and separated them.

Upon separating the two boys, it was apparent that one of them – Benjamin – was far more aggressive than the other. He was cussing at both myself and my colleague, and at the other boy, and making threats. The first thing we did was to warn Benjamin to calm down. He did not heed this advice, and if anything he became more aggressive. He tried to throw a punch at my colleague. Our immediate action following this was to restrain him. The other boy was sitting there quietly, and did not seem to be an issue. Ultimately, Benjamin would not calm down, and we were forced to arrest him for his aggressive behaviour.

I believe that my colleague and I acted in a professional fashion, that was in full coordination with the expectations and requirements of the police service. I'm pleased with the way we behaved.

Sincerely,

PC Watkins

Q4.

Answer

Dear Wendy,

Thank you so much for looking after Pickles while I'm away. I know he'll be well looked after at the cattery, and I really hope he behaves for you! In order to make sure everything goes smoothly, I've provided a couple of bits of important information which should prove useful.

In terms of diet, Pickles' preference is for MeatyCat sachets – 1 full packet in the morning and 1 full packet in the afternoon. He likes to eat at 8am for breakfast, and 4pm for dinner. In terms of flavour, he isn't too fussy, but he will not touch salmon – so I would avoid giving him this. Usually, Pickles goes to bed at 11pm, and then wakes up around 7am. However, his bedtimes are flexible, and he's not too fussy here.

Pickles is generally a well-behaved cat, but there are times when he goes a bit crazy! Specifically, at 5pm and 9pm he will be bouncing off the walls, and you can expect him to be running around like a mad cat during those hours. He'll hide around the corner and then jump out at you, expecting you to chase him. If you don't indulge him then he will calm down, but if you do play then don't worry, he won't use his claws!

Q5.

Answer

Dear Frederick,

Thank you very much for your letter, and I'm glad to hear that things are going so well for you. Unfortunately, things aren't so great here. I recently got fired from my job – after I accidentally set the staff kitchen on fire. Although nobody was hurt, and it was a total accident, the boss said this was the last straw. I'm sad to lose my job, but I'm sure I can find another one…

I've recently been spending a lot of time at the gym, but I'm finding it very difficult to maintain my discipline and keep it up. I'm not in the best shape, but I made a vow to myself that I will lose at least some of this weight.

It's great to hear about your family. My family is all good. My sister just graduated from university, and she's going to be a doctor soon – so that makes two doctors in the family!

Hope to hear from you soon,

Mikey.

Q6.

Answer

Dear Mr Fudley,

I am writing to you today to inform you that unfortunately I am handing in my resignation. After three years at this company, I believe that now is the right time to move on.

The reasons for my resignation are plentiful, but mainly I am leaving because I do not like the direction that this organisation is taking. On many occasions I have brought up the clear evidence of one of our board members, Mrs Morgan, embezzling funds from the company – but it appears that nobody wants to confront this issue. This has been happening for several months now, and I just can't believe the ignorance being shown. Furthermore, with numerous cuts taking place within the company, I feel we have lost some incredibly vital staff members, and retained certain members of staff who add nothing to the company.

I do not have any plans to work for a competing company, as per my contract, but in the future I will be considering working within a similar field. I thought it was important for me to point this out, as I don't want to leave on a sour note.

I have enjoyed working for this company for the past 3 years, but I can simply no longer continue.

Sincerely,

Marvin.

Q7.

Answer

Dear Mrs Wibbley,

I am writing to you to complain about the service I received from your restaurant. I am appalled by the way that my husband and I were treated by the staff.

When we arrived at the restaurant, we were seated next to the window. My husband had specifically requested that we weren't placed near a window – as he suffers from paranoia and is afraid of potential gunmen. When I pointed this out to the waitress, she simply laughed in my face. So, we took our seats…feeling deeply uncomfortable.

Eventually, after almost half an hour, another waiter approached me to take our order. I was promptly informed that there was none of the meat I wanted on the menu, and my husband didn't get what he wanted either. When the food eventually arrived, it was stone cold, and absolutely disgusting. My husband called the waiter over and informed him that 'my meal tastes like dog food.' The waiter sneered at him, and walked away.

I would like to see an investigation made into the quality of the food, the service we received, and to receive a refund and an explanation for this incident. It's simply not acceptable.

Sincerely,

Marianne Wiggins.

Q8.

Answer

Dear Mr Gildsworth,

I am writing today to request a formal meeting, ideally with you and your son. I am Kevin's English teacher. Unfortunately Kevin's behaviour in my lessons has become incredibly disruptive, and I can no longer allow things to continue as they are. Kevin's behaviour seems to have rapidly deteriorated in the last few months. In the lesson today he sat at the back of the room throwing rubbers at my head and at his classmates. When I asked him to stop, he refused. Other incidences include going behind my back and drawing inappropriate images on the board, stabbing classmates with a compass, and even encouraging the class to hide underneath their desks – in apparent anticipation of a bomb scare.

As mentioned, I simply can't allow this to continue. Not only is Kevin making it impossible for me to teach, but he's disrupting the learning of all of his other classmates. I believe that we need to get to the bottom of this issue, together, and work out a way in which Kevin can amend his behaviour.

I will be available to meet with yourself and Kevin on any Tuesday over the next month, after 5pm. Please let me know whether this is suitable.

Kind regards,

Professor Winchurch.

Q9.

Answer

Dear Paul,

I am the current resident of flat A431, in Pimsbury Block. I'm writing to draw your attention to a number of issues that have arisen in the flat. As the landlord of this property, I would really appreciate your assistance in fixing these issues, as none of them are my responsibility.

The first problem I am having is that there appears to be no consistency to my water temperature. The water goes from freezing to boiling within less than 30 seconds, and then back again. As you can imagine, this makes showering a very uncomfortable experience.

Secondly, there appears to be a colony of rats living underneath my bedroom floor. I can hear them at night, rattling around. I am terrified of rats, so this needs immediate attention.

Thirdly, and more seriously, somebody keeps breaking into my flat. Every time I leave the flat, I come back to find posters of a prominent boy band festooned all over my walls. It is not me that is doing this – and I am highly disturbed. I would like you to place CCTV cameras in the corridor, at the very least.

I am available to meet at any time after 5pm, Monday to Friday. Please contact me at your earliest convenience.

Kind regards,

Molly.

Q10.

Answer

Dear Mrs Everett,

I am writing to you today to ask for some advice. As you know, I was recently placed in charge of the customer service team. Unfortunately, I've been having some issues with two members of my group, and I'd like your advice on how to deal with this.

The first member of my team is named Kyle. Kyle is a new employee, and as such appears to be having trouble grasping the core concept of 'customer facing behaviour.' Last week I saw him pick his nose in front of a customer, and several customers have complained about Kyle's flatulence. When I questioned him about this, he said, 'It's just human nature.' Obviously, this cannot continue.

The second member of my team is named Jenny. Jenny has been with the company for a while, and it appears that she is harbouring extreme resentment over my promotion. Other staff members have informed me that Jenny 'swore revenge on me'. Last week I discovered that someone had slashed my tyres in the car park at work. I cannot prove that it was Jenny, but I have my suspicions. I've tried talking to her, but she says that she's always busy.

I believe that these problems are occurring because Kyle and Jenny have a serious lack of respect for me. I would like your advice on how to deal with this, please.

Sincerely,

Janet.

Q11.

Answer

Dear Mr Steel,

I am writing today to complain about the train services this morning, on the 13/07/2018. I cannot believe the sheer incompetence of Ficshire Rail, and I would really like some compensation.

To explain further, this morning I was due to catch a train to Northbury, at 8:12am. I had an extremely important meeting at work at half past. Unfortunately, my train was cancelled. And the next one was too. There was absolutely no explanation for why this was the case from the station announcements. 30 minutes later, after paying £15 for a return ticket, I got onto a train which had no available seats – so was forced to stand in the sweltering heat. This is outrageous. How can you charge me £15 for a 10-minute journey, and then not even guarantee a seat? I have not received any apology from any member of Ficshire Rail staff, and missing my work meeting has caused me a great deal of problems.

I would like to know what you will be doing to compensate me for this issue. At the very least, I would like reimbursement for my ticket.

Sincerely,

Mick.

Q12.

Answer

Dear Professor Minchin,

I am writing to you to apologise profusely for my late submission. Unfortunately I have missed the submission deadline, and now I will need to submit the final essay tomorrow – first thing at 9am. The reason I missed the deadline was because I had a family emergency. This was totally unexpected. Obviously I would rather not openly discuss personal information, but my sister was forced to go into hospital, and is still in very bad condition. With this in mind, I hope you will understand the extenuating circumstances behind this, and I hope that my late submission is acceptable.

Whilst there are extenuating circumstances behind this, I do understand that my own poor time management is also at fault here and that I should have had this piece of work completed earlier than yesterday. With this in mind, I can only apologise, and assure you that I have learned for next time.

Sincerely,

Miranda.

Q13.

Answer

Dear Mrs Perkins,

I am writing to you to explore the implications of the data leak – which has impacted our company so majorly this week. I am doing everything in my power to find out who is responsible for this, including interviewing people from the department that the leak originated from – Accounting and Finance. Thus far, every single person is proclaiming their innocence, but I believe we are narrowing down on the source.

In regards to resolving the problem, we have placed hard restrictions from any person from the company talking to the media, and an injunction has been placed against any potential news reports discussing the leak.

We are already in the process of establishing a system that will ensure something like this cannot happen again, with only certain people in the company chain being given access to restrictive information, and the system logging the access usage of every single person.

Rest assured, we will resolve this situation, and find the persons responsible.

Sincerely,

Jason Smith.

Q14.

Answer

Dear Becky,

Thank you so much for inviting us to your wedding. We had such an amazing time. Everything was beautiful, and we were particularly impressed by the harpist and ice sculpture. You must have spent a fortune on all that, but totally worth it! The ceremony itself was really lovely, and it was so good to see you and Wendy finally tie the knot. Couldn't be happier for you guys, and we really hope you enjoy your honeymoon.

Just one thing to note, which might be of concern to you guys: we met a woman at the party who was quite drunk. She kept telling me (and everyone else) that you stole her wife, and that she was going to 'do something about it'. Not sure what that means, but watch out for her! I don't know her name sadly.

Once you get back from your honeymoon we should meet up for a drink. Would July the 20th work for you?

Speak to you soon, have a great time away.

Martha.

Q15.

Answer

Dear Patrick,

I am writing to you in response to your proposal for The Carlton Building to host our company event. We would be very pleased to consider this location. Before we make anything definite though, it's important that I let you know about the specifications for the event.

We will need a venue which has seating capacity for 350 people, and 100 people standing. 20 of our guests have specific seating requirements, for spinal conditions, so will need padded, leather seating. The venue must have 3 toilets, 2 fire exits, and a space where attendees can eat. The venue should not serve alcohol.

As a company, we are willing to pay a maximum of £5000 for the venue booking, but ideally we will be looking for venues in the price range of £4000-£4200.

I really hope that we can come to an agreement on this, and I look forward to hearing back from you on whether The Carlton Building can satisfy these requirements.

Sincerely,

Mark Edwards.

Q16.

Answer

In my opinion, students should be made to exercise. There is a bevy of scientific evidence to support the fact that a lack of early exercise leads to problems such as obesity and diabetes, and therefore it's imperative that schools play an active role in ironing this out. The problem is not with PE itself, but with the way PE lessons are run, and the type of exercise that children are being made to perform. Can you really blame children for not wanting to run 1500m around a track, in below 0 temperatures? Coupled with the fact that most school PE uniforms consist of tiny shorts and a thin top, it's no surprise that children are reluctant.

Furthermore, Britain has a growing obesity problem, and it's up to schools to stamp this out early. Statistics show that if we don't take a stand now, obesity rates will roar by 2030. In the USA alone, it is estimated that at least half the population will be obese unless something is done. Britain faces a similar issue. Doctors have highlighted a 30% increase in the rise of obesity in England alone, within the last 20 years. If we don't act soon; it will be far too late.

From my own personal experience, I didn't enjoy exercising at school initially, but once I actually got into it I really had fun. I think that sometimes the idea of exercising is scary for children, and they just need a little push in the right direction. Schools are responsible for the wellbeing of our children during the day, and this includes looking after their physical health.

Q17.

Answer

Gun control is an interesting topic, and I am firmly in favour of stricter rules surrounding weapons.

One of the most commonly cited reasons for carrying weapons, from pro-gun activists, is that people have a right to defend themselves against the government. These people are, quite frankly, deluded. In the unlikely event that the government did decide to turn against its citizens, a handgun would not be much use. The government has tanks, drones, planes and bombs at its disposal. Unless these people would change the law to allow all citizens access to rocket launchers and other heavy weaponry, they will have to reconcile themselves with the uncomfortable truth that a physical resistance against the US Government would be virtually impossible.

Equally as ridiculous is the argument that gun control laws violate the second amendment. The second amendment states, 'a well-regulated militia being necessary to the security of the Free State, the right of the people to keep and bear Arms shall not be infringed'. This is all well and good, if you ignore the power of the US military. Is it really necessary to have a citizen based military, just to ensure American sovereignty? The US military is the strongest armed force in the world.

The majority of studies have shown that gun laws reduce violence. Some people argue that it's not guns that kill people, it is people that kill people. That might be true, but people with guns kill more people than they would if they didn't have guns. For this reason, I believe that we need to place more emphasis on the regulation of firearms, and that tighter controls are needed.

Q18.

Answer

Whilst I agree with the principle behind ethical veganism, I believe there are real questions over how ethical it actually is.

Firstly, while refusing to consume products which are associated with animal cruelty is certainly an ethical decision, it carries implications which aren't so moral. For these reasons, ethical veganism isn't as morally valuable as a vegan would have you believe. For example, a vegan diet in the modern Western world consists of a range of products, many of which aren't seasonal. Thanks to globalisation, the entire world is a web of train, plane, and boat links, allowing for people to get all kinds of fruit, vegetables, and other products that are suitable for vegans to eat. While this means that vegans can enjoy a varied and balanced diet, it also has negative impacts on the world. The carbon footprint caused by importing from across the globe must be disastrous. So, an ethical vegan directly contributes to climate change.

The second major moral dilemma worth discussing is as much an issue with capitalism in general as it is ethical veganism specifically. In order to meet the demands of a vegan population, a significant number of farmhands are necessary to work the land. To keep the costs of these products as low as possible, these labourers are often paid poorly and work under uncomfortable conditions. In some cases, it has been suggested that the labourers are mostly migrant workers who are being exploited for the gain of wealthy people in Western countries. So, this means that the ethical vegan implicitly endorses the exploitation of human beings, so long as animals are safe and looked after.

In conclusion, I do not believe that ethical veganism is truly ethical, and that there are a number of factors, including human exploitation, which count against this view.

Q19.

Answer

I believe that patriotism is a flawed concept, with a number of issues. These are as follows:

Firstly, I would argue that patriotism is subconsciously xenophobic. We are all members of the human race, and are no different to one another. Countries are just arbitrary borders designed to enforce the idea that English are different from Spanish, Italians from Germans etc. This is not healthy, and often leads to a severe clash of cultures. Human beings are human beings, regardless of where on the Earth they reside.

Although there is a difference between patriotism and nationalism, patriotism breeds nationalism. By enforcing an unnecessary and unhealthy idea that people of one nation are different from those of another, we generate tension between countries, which leads to a sense of hatred from disenchanted individuals. This results in extremist behaviour, and accelerates global conflicts.

Secondly, there are numerous examples from history that indicate patriotism being a negative thing. Primary amongst these is the world wars. In particular World War 2 was caused by extreme national pride (in Germany). Combined with severe social unrest, this led to an uprising which resulted in the deaths of millions of people.

You could also argue that despite the success of events such as the World Cup, there is still an underlying xenophobia prevalent from the citizens of each nation towards other nations. i.e. the English are rooting against the Italians, or the Germans, or the Spanish. Such events could easily be held without this. Often, it leads to people who aren't patriotic being ostracised or treated as traitors. This is not healthy.

In conclusion, I believe that patriotism is a fundamentally flawed concept, which subconsciously encourages people to foster resentment or animosity towards other, based simply on what country they come from. The country you are born in is ultimately down to chance, so why celebrate this?

Q20.

Answer

While I personally enjoy using social media, I think it's fair to say that there are a great number of risks associated with this, which must be taken into account.

Firstly, there is the fact that information posted on these sites is likely to come back and haunt a person in the future. Just think of a social networking site as a type of "global database". You are posting information, facts about yourself, images etc, into your very own "database", acting as a log of your personal behaviour for others to view. This is a great concern for many parents, whereby they feel obliged to check how secure their child is whilst they're online.

An example of the impact of social networking occurred in America, whereby students were faced with court charges for underage drinking, a situation that had it not been shared on their social networking profiles, would never have been known otherwise. The students in question were unaware of the impact of their behaviour of underage drinking and posting the evidence online.

Social media sites are also becoming an increasing concern in terms of bullying, grooming and abuse. With a small minority of users utilising the security system to its fullest, profiles are subsequently left open to everyone. A profile can be used to track down someone, find out what someone is up to, stalk an individual, and become somewhat obsessive over the lives of other people.

In conclusion, I do believe that social media sites can be seen as dangerous – for all of the reasons listed above, but I do not think that social media is dangerous by nature, given that it was created in part to connect people from all over the world in a positive manner.

Q21.

Answer

Fake news can be defined as 'a type of journalism which focuses on deliberate dissemination of misinformation and hoaxes – usually to serve an agenda.' I believe that fake news is harmful to society. The primary reason for this is as follows:

Our modern social and technological landscape makes fake news a bigger threat than ever. The most important angle we need to examine is how technology and society have merged over the past ten years or so. The dramatic rise of social media, forums, online video gaming, and other platforms have led the internet to become a fragmented place, split into countless communities. Those who wish to spread fake news can infect these fragmented communities. Without a unified society to watch over each other's shoulders, hoax-spreaders can get to work on manipulating different subsets of internet society into essentially working for them.

Whether these subcultures are inherently political or not is irrelevant: all it takes is an opportunistic group of propagandists to convince a subset of internet society that a political event matters to them. From there, the community can be convinced to spread false information on the propagandists' behalf. The very nature of modern social media means that it's incredibly easy to spread false information. All it takes is a credible-looking thumbnail image and hyperlink, combined with a sensationalist headline, for misinformation to swell across the internet.

Fake news can bound its way across the internet, and since many people don't think to corroborate the information, what was once nonsense is now accepted as fact.

In conclusion, I believe that fake news, and spreading misinformation, is extremely harmful. As a society, we should seek the truth, and strongly discourage the spread of lies and falsities.

Q22.

Answer

I believe that not having met someone should not be used as an excuse for displaying a lack of morals towards that person, and that as members of the human race we have a duty of care and responsibility for each other.

The primary reason I believe this is as follows:

Let's take an example of someone we will never meet, but certainly have a moral connection with. Most of our clothes in the Western world are produced in South and South-East Asia. The people who work in the factories that manufacture these garments are often paid quite poorly, at least by Western standards. This is one of the ways in which retailers can sell clothes for much cheaper. So, when we save money by buying cheap clothes, this is as a result of potentially exploited workers in foreign countries. Essentially, the cheap pair of jeans you bought only exist because someone in a faraway land is underpaid.

We benefit from their exploitation, but do we have a moral obligation to them? I'll never meet the people in Sri Lanka who stitched my shirt together, so why should I care about them? Based on this argument I should save my "moral energy" for those closer to me, and leave the worrying about disadvantaged people overseas to their own friends and family.

The principal issue with this mode of thinking is that it doesn't demonstrate a clear cut-off point for where you should stop caring about people. I should care about myself, my immediate family, friends, and extended family – this is fairly uncontroversial. However, what about my family's friends, or my friends' families? Are they outside of my apathy wall? The answer is no.

In conclusion, I believe that we have a responsibility as human beings to care for each other. Any statement which claims that we shouldn't, fails to take into account our moral code, and fails to address the complex social webs built into relationship concepts such as family, or even distant family.

Q23.

Answer

It's undeniable that war is a terrible thing, and that most people would argue that the world would be better off without conflict, but I do not believe that we can completely discredit war as pure evil. There are a few ways in which war has actually helped the human race to progress.

Firstly, there are numerous technological and medical advancements which would never have been made were it not for warfare. Penicillin likely wouldn't have been mass-produced were it not for the Second World War, which would mean that the modern world would lack vital antibiotics. Likewise, the x-ray machine was developed because of its usefulness in diagnosing wounds during the First World War. Were it not for the Second World War and the allied powers' bombings of Hiroshima and Nagasaki, we might not have developed nuclear energy. If necessity is the mother of invention, then war is the greatest inventor of them all.

Technological advancements aside, war and conflict can lead to social and political progress. Organisations such as the United Nations were established as a result of the Second World War, ushering in an era of globalised economies and political structures. The Second World War also ended in the destruction of the Nazis as a global power. This is surely a cause for celebration.

So, it's clear that war is far from a good thing overall. However, to completely dismiss the positive outcomes of war, and how much our modern world has benefitted from it, would be incredibly naïve.

Q24.

Answer

I believe that human beings have had a massive impact on the planet. In many cases, our actions are reckless and have caused irreparable damage to the Earth. Our actions far outweigh those of any natural causes.

Burning fossil fuels is a clear example of how, over the past 15 decades, human beings have impacted the environment. The world has become more industrialised and changed the balance of the carbon cycle. Burning fossil fuels such as oil, gas and coal converts carbon into carbon dioxide, and unless it is captured, the carbon dioxide is released into the atmosphere. This climate change is characterised by higher than average global temperatures and the increased sea levels.

Forests have a huge role to play in fighting climate change. Forests can be used to absorb and store carbon in their soil and trees. Yet, we continue to cut these forests down with no hindsight of the consequences that follow. Why? Why do we continue these actions if we know what the outcome and consequences are going to be?

If these forests are frequently being cut down, then all the stored emissions from the trees, will be released into the atmosphere. Up to one fifth of greenhouse gas emissions comes from deforestation and forest degradation, which indicates the scale of the issue and the impact it causes in terms of global warming.

Some people consider global warming as "natural", yet it is apparent that we, as the contributing factors to climate change, need to change our behaviour. Science tells us that although the Earth's climate has always changed, our actions in the way we have treated our planet remain the most damaging.

Q25.

Answer

Many people believe that violence, conflict, and evil are intertwined. Violence is a central part of ethics, with violent behaviour generally being considered immoral. While this is mostly true, it's also a slight simplification of how the world really works.

Ideally, all conflict in the world would be avoided altogether, and we should continue to strive for a conflict-free world. Until then, however, there will always be those who use violence as a means of disorder. Sometimes, the only way to prevent this violence is through more violence: albeit more targeted, skilful, and measured. The only way to destroy a terror cell might be to kill its leader, or at least use violent means of capturing them.

However, there are a few issues with this line of reasoning. Firstly, is it possible to create a peaceful world through conflict? Wars have been fought for righteous, "peace-making" causes for hundreds (if not thousands) of years, yet we are still faced with more violence and conflict. Using violence as a means of creating less violence is clearly ineffective, and therefore it shouldn't be justified on utilitarian grounds.

Moreover, there's no reason to believe that it is only guilty people who have been killed in these peace-keeping efforts. We should also consider who we are giving the power to decide who lives and who dies to. Surely the only person who would desire such a responsibility is someone who is bloodthirsty, and therefore they are more likely to permit violence towards innocents. However, someone who is more measured is less likely to want the position. This means that the people who are employed to make these decisions are always the worst people to do so. Therefore, violence is not justified.

General Training Reading: About the Test

The IELTS General Training reading assessment will examine candidates' ability to read through texts of varying length and difficulty, and then answer questions based on these texts. It's very similar to the Academic reading, with the difference being that the texts chosen will be different in nature, and the question types will be slightly different too.

The test will last for 1 hour in total, and there will be 40 questions. The questions are designed to tested elements such as:

- How well you can identify information after reading a text.

- How well you can understand a writer's views and opinions.

- How efficiently you can 'skim read'.

- How well you can understand logic and arguments for/against the text.

- How much detail you can remember, having read a text.

There are three sections to the IELTS General Training reading assessment, and these are as follows:

Social Survival

The first section is called social survival. This section contains a variety of texts, which focus on linguistic English survival. For example, reading timetables, safety manuals, or advertisements.

Workplace Survival

The second section is called workplace survival. The texts in this section are set in a workplace context. For example, staff training guides, job descriptions, training manuals and behavioural instructions for the workplace.

General Reading

The third section is called general reading, where you will be required to read a piece of extended prose, with a more complicated structure than the previous texts. The prose could be from a book, magazine, newspaper, or other fictional and non-fictional forms of media.

Each question is worth 1 mark, and there are a variety of question types. The question types that you will see are the same as they are in the Academic Reading, which can be found on page 82. Now, have a go at our practice questions!

General Training Reading: Practice Questions

Social Survival

Is your home dirty? Do you ever find yourself cursing your rusty, worn out vacuum cleaner? If so, we've got the perfect solution for you!

The "Vroom Voom 5000" is the ULTIMATE cleaning accessory for any self-respecting house owner. Fitted with anti-allergen technology and a high-tech filter, the Voom hoover will leave your house looking fit for a king. The Voom comes complete with:

-THREE accessible cleaning modes. Easy to use, just flick the switch on the side to choose the mode you want. Choose from Hardcore Clean, Intermediate Sweep and Soft Swipe.

-EIGHT different hoover brushes, each one with their own unique and interesting function.

-TWO interchangeable filters. When one gets dirty, all you have to do is swap it out!

-ONE spectacular engine. The Voom drives faster than 98% of hoovers on the market. Accelerate the process of cleaning, and get around to the things you really want to do.

You'll love the Voom so much that you'll never want to put it down. And on top of this, we offer a 30-day partial money back guarantee! Don't like it? No problem. Just get in touch with us and we'll offer you a refund.

Don't waste time. Pick up your Vroom Voom 5000 TODAY, for just £600.50

Terms and conditions

Voom LTD cannot be held responsible for any injury that befalls any person using the Vroom Voom 5000. Partial Refunds are available but customers will need to prove that the Voom did not meet their expectations. Full refunds are not available and Voom LTD will not consider providing these. Voom LTD are aware of a number of models exploding upon activation, but do not take any responsibility for this or injury that results from usage. Customers who purchase online will be subject to a recurring payment of £200 per month following the initial payment of £600.50, for 60 days following purchase.

Look at the following statements, and work out whether they correspond with the information given in the passage. Your answer options are as follows:

TRUE. You should only select this if the statement can be verified by the passage.

FALSE. You should only select this if the statement contradicts the information in the passage.

IMPOSSIBLE TO SAY. You should only select this if the passage does not give enough information on the statement for it to be verified as true or false.

Q1. The Vroom Voom 5000 would be a good solution for owners who suffer from hayfever.

TRUE	FALSE	IMPOSSIBLE TO SAY

Q2. In order to change the cleaning mode on the Vroom Voom 5000, the user needs to push a button located on the underside of the hoover.

TRUE	FALSE	IMPOSSIBLE TO SAY

Q3. Customers who purchase the Vroom Voom 5000 will pay a one-time fee, of £600.50.

TRUE	FALSE	IMPOSSIBLE TO SAY

Q4. Customers who aren't happy with the Voom will receive a full refund.

TRUE	FALSE	IMPOSSIBLE TO SAY

Q5. The voom comes in red, blue, silver and gold colours.

TRUE	FALSE	IMPOSSIBLE TO SAY

ATTENTION FOR CUSTOMERS:

From the 1st July 2018, Ficshire Rail will be undergoing enormous new changes. We've got fresh new timetables, new trains and new prices coming.

Due to the completion of South Ficshire Bridge, Ficshire Rail can finally traverse the route from North Ficshire to South Ficshire again. This brings many new opportunities for customers, and for this reason we are re-doing the whole timetable. From the 1st July onwards, the following routes will have drastically changed timetables:

-North Ficshire to South Ficshire, stopping at Tramley Brook, Harring Gate, Eastshire, terminating at South Ficshire.

-North Ficshire to Kemley West, stopping at South Ficshire, Eastwood, Longington, Hamley Marsh, terminating at Kemley West.

-North Ficshire to Primrose Village, stopping at Tramley Brook, South Ficshire, Longington, Kemley West, Eastmoore, Owl's Keep, terminating at Primrose Village.

-North Ficshire to Stone Valley, stopping at Tramley Moore, Harring Gate, South Ficshire, Kemley West, Owl's Keep, Broadshire, terminating at Stone Valley.

Go to www.FicshireRail.com to see how YOUR timetable has changed. Don't get caught out by the NEW rail changes coming your way this summer.

On top of the timetable changes, Ficshire Rail is also introducing brand new improved trains to your line. All our new trains will have one extra toilet, and there will be three extra seats on each train. There'll also be MORE first-class seating available on every single train. If you enjoy travelling in luxury, then you are in for a treat.

To fund this INCREDIBLE new improvement, we're changing our prices ever so slightly. All individual and season ticket prices will be increased by just 40%. That's right, just 40% for one brand spanking new toilet in almost IEVERY single Ficshire Rail train. If that sounds great, then prepare to have your socks knocked off – because we're also increasing security. We've spent the spring season training our ticket inspectors in the art of security, and now you'll see lots more of them on your trains – keeping you safe and sound.

We look forward to receiving your feedback once the rail changes go live.

Sincerely,

The Ficshire Rail Team.

Q6. Completing the missing words in the following paragraph

Ficshire Rail are finally able to travel to South Ficshire again, due to the completion of a … . This means that routes from North Ficshire all the way to ……… will be altered, with new timetable changes coming into effect from 1st of ……. Ficshire Rail are also putting new ……. in their trains.

A – viaduct, Owl's Keep, August, cameras.

B – railway track, Tramley, June, fire doors.

C – bridge, Stone Valley, July, toilets.

D – signalling house, Owl's Keep, January, air conditioning units.

E – warehouse, Eastmoore, September, leather seats.

F – gateway, Longington, February, fire extinguishers.

G – ticket machine, Kemley West, April, doors.

Q7. Customers from which of the following stations are not impacted by the timetable changes?

A – Owl's Keep

B – Westshire

C – Harring Gate

D – Hamley Marsh

Q8. Which of the following do Ficshire Rail use to justify their price increase?

A – The increased revenue will be used to provide extra leg room for people in first class carriages.

B – The increased revenue will be used to put new toilets in every single train.

C – The increased revenue will be used to enhance the number of seats on every single train.

D – The increased revenue will be used to facilitate the cleaning costs of Ficshire Rail train carriages.

E – The increased revenue will be used to facilitate the costs of travelling further distances.

F – The increased revenue will be used to line the pockets of Ficshire Rail executives.

G – The increased revenue will be used to solve the financial problems of the Ficshire Rail chairman.

Q9. On the route from North Ficshire to Stone Valley, which of the following stations comes after Kemley West?

A – Owl's Keep

B – South Ficshire

C – Primrose Village

D – Longington

Q10. Based on the passage, which of the following are you encouraged to assume?

A – The fact that the Ficshire Rail prices increase coincides with extra ticket inspectors on the trains is a mere coincidence.

B – The extra ticket inspectors on trains are not just there to help provide security.

C – The extra ticket inspectors on trains take a commission from the increased fares.

D – The extra ticket inspectors on trains take pleasure in fining unfortunate commuters.

E – The fact that the Ficshire Rail prices have increased is actually a good thing for customers.

Message From North Ficshire Council

Dear Residents,

We're writing to you all today with some very exciting news. From the 2nd August onwards, construction will begin on a brand-new theme park, right in the heart of North Ficshire. The theme park will be called Shark World, and every ride and attraction will be based around the Sharks that live in the waters of Ficshire Bay. We expect the park to be finished sometime late next year, and it will then open for the following summer – so start planning your trips for Summer 2020!

When fully constructed, the theme park will contain over one hundred exciting new rides, suitable for children and adults alike. The park owners and Ficshire council have already established ticket prices, opening hours, and base attractions, which we've listed below:

Standard Rates

1 x regular Adult ticket (16+) 8 hours at park = £62.50

1 x regular Child ticket, 8 hours at park = £32.50

One regular ticket gives you full access to the park, unlimited access to all of the rides, for the duration of an 8-hour stay. Visitors to the park will be required to wear their ticket on their wrist. Any person found staying in the park beyond their applicated time will be escorted from the premises by security, and asked to pay a fine.

FAST TRACK TICKETS = £265 for Adults, £150 for children.

Fast track your Shark experience, at great prices! Fast track tickets give you the chance to skip the queue for ONE ride of your choosing, with the exception of The Big Fin 2. On top of this, fast track tickets provide you with a 2% discount in the gift shop.

The Big Fin...2

Get ready for the ride of your life, as you experience THE BIG FIN...2. That's right, we've teamed up with the creators of the original Big Fin ride over in South Ficshire, to bring you the SECOND edition of this ultimate shark experience. Climb into the tank with REAL sharks, and experience what it's like to swim side by side with a real Great White. Stare into the pearly white jaws of the king of the ocean, with no cage to protect you! Will you survive your experience with Jacques, our French Great White?! Please see our terms and conditions for more information.

Terms and conditions

Shark World accepts no responsibility for any person who comes to harm whilst on any of the rides at the theme park. Furthermore, Shark World offers no guarantee that the trainers provided to assist children and adults on The Big Fin 2 are capable of dealing with aggressive marine behaviour. All participants do so at their own risk, and Shark World cannot guarantee the safety of marine life or visitors to the park. Please note there is no capacity for first aid at Shark World, and therefore visitors will need to make their own way to the hospital in event of emergency.

Q11. Based on the advertisement, which of the following is true?

A – Adult customers to Shark World can fast track their experience for £260. When fast tracking, customers are given a 2% discount in the gift shop.

B – Customers to Shark World are offered no guarantee of protection or first aid by the park.

C – Shark World requires customers to wear a necklace displaying their ticket, lest they be escorted from the premises by the park security.

D – The Big Fin 2 gives customers the chance to swim with dolphins and killer whales.

E – The park is being funded by a millionaire, who has recently invested large amounts of money into marine life.

F – The park will provide Ficshire with enormous new investment and tourism.

G – The park will be the central hub of Ficshire's new retail estate.

Q12. Based on the advertisement, which of the following statements is true?

A – Visitors to Shark World are expected to conduct hourly litter patrols, tidying up any and all mess that they see.

B – Visitors to Shark World are encouraged to bring along an experienced swimmer, especially if they plan on experiencing The Big Fin 2.

C – Visitors to Shark World can swim with Stringrays and Jellyfish.

D – Visitors to Shark World will not receive compensation from the park if they are injured whilst there.

E – Visitors to Shark World are under no obligation to pay the entrance fee.

Q13. Complete the missing word in the below sentence:

Shark World visitors will incur the wrath of security if they stay beyond their allocated time slot. The consequence of such behaviour is that they will be asked to …… .

A – Spend the night in jail.

B – Spend an hour in the tank with Jacques the Great White.

C – Pay a fine.

D – Perform community service at the park.

E – Be banned from visiting the park ever again.

Q14. The park owners are working with which of the following bodies, to construct the amusement park?

A – The mayor of Ficshire.

B – The queen of England.

C – The council of North Ficshire.

D – The guardians of Ficshire.

E – The Ficshire marine life society.

Q15. Complete the missing words in the below paragraph:

A new marine amusement park is being built in ………. . The park will have over ………. rides and offer visitors the unique chance to swim with a ….. without any safety barrier. The park does not guarantee the safety of its visitors, so entrants come at their own …..

A – South Ficshire, two hundred, dolphin, precaution.

B – Westshire, three hundred, Stingray, wellbeing.

C – South Ficshire, one hundred, shark, presumption.

D – North Ficshire, one hundred, shark, risk.

Workplace Survival

EMPLOYEE BEHAVIOUR AND WORKPLACE GUIDE

To all our new employees,

Welcome, and we are so pleased to have you here at our new company – Marketing Gurus incorporated. From myself and Kevin, the cog on which this whole company turns, we are grateful that you've decided to join us.

As I'm sure you'll already be aware, our main aim as a company is to make as much money as possible, by selling our patented marketing products to customers throughout the UK. To do this, we have a wide range of products available:

- Various CDs and DVDs, selling our marketing-based ideas to the general public.

- Books, selling the same ideas as above.

- Various T-shirts and mugs, which can be purchased from our online gift shop.

- Special course days, where customers will have the opportunity to meet Kevin, our lord and saviour in these troubled marketing times.

Telephone Conduct

Since I know many of you will be manning the complaints telephone line as part of your new job, it's important to explain some key things about our code of telephone conduct. Here at Marketing Gurus, we understand that you'll try your best to help everyone. That's why, when somebody calls us with a complaint, we do our best to assist them in every way, shape or form. It's only £0.50 a minute for people to call our phones, but here at Marketing Gurus we generously make sure that every customer is getting the best level of service possible, for the longest time possible. After all, time is extremely valuable.

From our experience, if you've got an angry customer, then the best way to deal with them is to keep them on the line until they've calmed down. A great way to do this is to use lots of buzzwords and phrases, such as: groundbreaking, entrepreneur, internet armageddon, unlimited wealth, goldrush and millionaire. What's more, when they ring you, our database actually collects their information – meaning we can market our fantastic products to them, time and time again. What better way to make up for our (rare) mistakes?

Here at Marketing Gurus Inc, we've got a 4-step system for dealing with telephone calls. It works like this:

- *The Introduction.* Greet the person on the end of the line, ask what they are calling for.

- *The Power of Positivity.* 99% of the time, what the customer is calling for is irrelevant. So, you need to turn the subject around.

Give them something you think they might be interested in, as a way of making them feel better. What do you think a customer would prefer to hear, that there's no refund for £5000 they spent on our business enhancement programme, or that we've got a great new product they might be interested in? Your job is to make their day better.

- *The Epiphany.* Now that you've got their attention, it's time to start talking. Tell them as much as you possibly can about the subject or product. Don't be afraid to repeat yourself.

- *The Long Goodbye.* Now you've finished talking about the product, it's time to try and convince them to purchase it. There's something important to remember here: no means yes. If you look at the company dictionary, published by Kevin himself, you won't even see the word no. It doesn't exist. It's just a word devised by negative people, to stop themselves falling into pre-conceived traps. Our customers want to buy our products, even if they don't know it. More than that, they *need* to buy our products. We know what's best for them.

No Refunds

Here at Marketing Gurus Incorporated, we don't do refunds. A refund is just a customer acknowledging that they didn't try hard enough with the product. It's for their own good that we say no. We want our customers to succeed, and if they are to succeed then they'll have to develop some determination. Don't let them give up.

Meeting Kevin

Occasionally, a customer or two will ring up demanding to speak directly to Kevin. Kevin spends most of his time in Hawaii at the moment, so he's not really around much, but as his team we are always here to help. Furthermore, if Kevin does visit the office, he does not appreciate being surrounded by eager new employees, desperate for words of wisdom. Keep your distance, and one day you might be as successful as Kevin himself.

We look forward to working with each and every one of you,

Sincerely,

Brian Morrison, Chief Executive of Marketing Gurus Inc

Look at the following statements, and work out whether they correspond with the information given in the passage. Your answer options are as follows:

TRUE. You should only select this if the statement can be verified by the passage.

FALSE. You should only select this if the statement contradicts the information in the passage.

IMPOSSIBLE TO SAY. You should only select this if the passage does not give enough information on the statement for it to be verified as true or false.

Q16. The main aim of Marketing Gurus Inc is to sell products to customers, through a telephone sales campaign.

TRUE	FALSE	IMPOSSIBLE TO SAY

Q17. Employees of the company are asked not to approach Kevin when he visits the office.

TRUE	FALSE	IMPOSSIBLE TO SAY

Q18. Brian Morrison is the Chief Executive of Marketing Gurus Inc. He is also a majority shareholder.

TRUE	FALSE	IMPOSSIBLE TO SAY

Q19. The four-step telephone plan was developed by Kevin himself.

TRUE	FALSE	IMPOSSIBLE TO SAY

Q20. Brian considers Kevin to be a figure of authority and importance.

TRUE	FALSE	IMPOSSIBLE TO SAY

Answer the following questions based on the passage.

Q21. Which of the following statements best summarises the intention of the author, Brian Morrison?

A – Brian has written this guide as a manual for new employees, on how to scam customers.

B – Brian has written this guide as a manual for new employees, so that they can understand the importance of Kevin to the company.

C – Brian has written this guide as a manual for new employees, so they can learn the way that Marketing Gurus Inc functions on a day-to-day basis.

D – Brian has written this guide as a manual for new employees, so that he does not get into trouble with the HR department.

Q22. Which of the following most accurately describes Brian's feelings towards customers?

A – Brian believes that Marketing Gurus Inc has a better understanding of what customers want, than the customer themselves.

B – Brian believes that the customers of Marketing Gurus Inc are fundamentally stupid, and should be treated as such.

C – Brian believes that the customers of Marketing Gurus Inc are an exploitable tool, to be milked for as much cash as possible.

D – Brian believes that Marketing Gurus Inc are providing a fundamentally decent and non-exploitative service to customers.

Q23. In the paragraph titled, 'The Power of Positivity', what is the central message that Brian is trying to put across?

A – It's better to sell more products to a customer, than give them a refund.

B – A customer would rather hear about new products, than be given a refund.

C – Marketing Gurus Inc customers would rather be told about new products, than be told that they won't receive a refund.

D – Brian does not want to give any customers any refunds.

Q24. Which of the following best explains Brian's logic for not giving refunds?

A – Brian believes that if a customer wants a refund, they simply haven't tried the product for long enough to be satisfied.

B – Brian believes that once someone pays for something, the seller is not obligated to return any money.

C – Brian believes that refunds are impossible, since the company spends the customer's money as soon as they get it.

D – Brian believes that the company has an obligation to help their customers achieve the best possible value for money.

Q25. In the context of the passage, which of the following most accurately describes the phrase 'time is money'?

A – Customers pay £0.50 a minute to call Marketing Gurus Inc, therefore the more time they spend on the phone the more money the company makes.

B – Marketing Gurus Inc employees should avoid spending time on the phone, as they are being paid to work, and this time could be better used elsewhere.

C – Brian Morrison is unhappy about having to take the time to write all of this out, as it has cost him money.

D – Marketing Gurus Inc considers their customer's time to be very valuable, and therefore they try to resolve telephone complaints as quickly as possible.

Q26. Brian instructs the new employees to use buzzwords, to appeal to customers. What do you think is the purpose of these buzzwords?

A – To persuade customers that Marketing Gurus Inc is a scam.

B – To entice customers to purchase more products, in the belief that they will become rich.

C – To persuade customers to stay on the phone, so that the team can resolve their complaint in an amicable fashion.

D – To persuade customers that an appointment with Kevin can make them rich beyond their wildest dreams.

General Reading

Alice's Adventures in Wonderland

1. There seemed to be no use in waiting by the little door, so she went back to the table, half hoping she might find another key on it, or at any rate a book of rules for shutting people up like telescopes: this time she found a little bottle on it, ('which certainly was not here before,' said Alice,) and round the neck of the bottle was a paper label with the words 'DRINK ME' beautifully printed on it in large letters.

2. It was all very well to say, 'Drink me,' but the wise, little Alice was not going to do that in a hurry. 'No I'll look first,' she said, 'and see whether it's marked "poison" or not:' for she had read several nice little histories about children who had got burnt, and eaten up by wild beasts and other unpleasant things, all because they would not remember the simple rules their friends had taught them: such as, that a red-hot poker will burn you if you hold it too long; and that if you cut your finger very deeply with a knife, it usually bleeds; and she had never forgotten that, if you drink much from a bottle marked 'poison,' it is almost certain to disagree with you, sooner or later.

3. However, this bottle was not marked 'poison,' so Alice ventured to taste it and finding it very nice, (it had, in fact, a sort of mixed flavour of cherry-tart, custard, pine-apple, roast turkey, toffee, and hot buttered toast,) she very soon finished it off.

4. 'What a curious feeling!' said Alice; 'I must be shutting up like a telescope.'

5. And so it was indeed: she was now only ten inches high, and her face brightened up at the thought that she was now the right size for going through the little door into that lovely garden. First, however, she waited for a few minutes to see if she was going to shrink any further: she felt a little nervous about this, 'for it might end, you know,' said Alice to herself, 'in my going out altogether like a candle. I wonder what I shall be like then?' And she tried to fancy what the flame of a candle is like after the candle is blown out, for she could not remember ever having seen such a thing.

6. After a while, finding that nothing more had happened, she decided on going into the garden at once; but alas for poor Alice! When she got to the door, she found she had forgotten the little golden key and when she went back to the table for it, she found she could not possibly reach it: she could see it quite plainly through the glass, and she tried her best to climb up one of the legs of the table, but it was too slippery; and when she had tired herself out with trying, the poor little thing sat down and cried.

7. 'Come, there's no use in crying like that!' said Alice to herself, rather sharply; 'I advise you to leave off this minute!' She generally gave herself very good advice, (though she very seldom followed it), and sometimes she scolded herself so severely as to bring tears into her eyes; and once she remembered trying to box her own ears for having cheated herself in a game of croquet she was playing against herself, for this curious child was very fond of pretending to be two people. 'But it's no use now,' thought poor Alice, 'to pretend to be two people! Why, there's hardly enough of me left to make one respectable person!'

Each of the paragraphs above has been assigned a number. Look at the following questions, and work out which paragraph they appear in.

Q27. Alice had forgotten the little golden key.

Q28. Alice compares herself to a telescope.

Q29. Bottles marked 'poison' will have a harmful impact on the body.

Q30. Alice rarely followed her own words of wisdom.

Q31. Alice failed to climb the leg of the table.

Q32. Alice often played a game where she would act like multiple people.

Look at the following statements, and work out whether they correspond with the information given in the passage. Your answer options are as follows:

TRUE. You should only select this if the statement can be verified by the passage.

FALSE. You should only select this if the statement contradicts the information in the passage.

IMPOSSIBLE TO SAY. You should only select this if the passage does not give enough information on the statement for it to be verified as true or false.

Q33. Alice generally gave herself poor advice.

TRUE	FALSE	IMPOSSIBLE TO SAY

Q34. Alice's mother boxed her ears, after she cheated in a game of croquet.

TRUE	FALSE	IMPOSSIBLE TO SAY

Q35. Alice was eleven years old.

TRUE	FALSE	IMPOSSIBLE TO SAY

Q36. Alice could not climb the leg of the table, as it was too slippery.

TRUE	FALSE	IMPOSSIBLE TO SAY

Q37. If you prick your finger with a needle, it will bleed.

TRUE	FALSE	IMPOSSIBLE TO SAY

Q38. Alice found another key on the table.

TRUE	FALSE	IMPOSSIBLE TO SAY

Q39. Poison is almost certain to disagree with you, sooner or later.

TRUE	FALSE	IMPOSSIBLE TO SAY

Q40. Alice's father died when she was young.

TRUE	FALSE	IMPOSSIBLE TO SAY

General Training
Reading: Answers

Q1. True

Q2. False

Q3. False

Q4. False

Q5. Impossible to Say

Q6. *Answer = C. bridge, Stone Valley, July, toilets.*

Explanation = Ficshire Rail are finally able to travel to South Ficshire again, due to the completion of a **bridge.** This means that routes from North Ficshire all the way to **Stone Valley** will be altered, with new timetable changes coming into effect from 1st of **July**. Ficshire Rail are also putting new **toilets** in their trains.

Q7. *Answer = B. Westshire.*

Explanation = Westshire is the only station on this list which does not appear in the passage.

Q8. *Answer = C. The increased revenue will be used to enhance the number of seats on every single train.*

Explanation = The passage states, '...there will be three extra seats on each train... To fund this INCREDIBLE new improvement, we're changing our prices ever so slightly.'

Q9. *Answer = A. Owl's Keep*

Explanation = Owl's Keep is the only station on this list which comes after Kemley West.

Q10. *Answer = A. The fact that the Ficshire Rail prices increase coincides with extra ticket inspectors on the trains is a mere coincidence.*

Explanation = The passage does not draw any link between the increased fares and the increase in ticket inspectors, instead inviting the conclusion that the ticket inspectors are there to provide security.

Q11. *Answer = B. Customers to Shark World are offered no guarantee of protection or first aid by the park.*

Explanation = The terms and conditions of the advert state, 'Shark World cannot guarantee the safety of marine life or visitors to the park. Please note there is no capacity for first aid at Shark World, and therefore visitors will need to make their own way to the hospital in event of emergency.'

Q12. Answer = D. Visitors to Shark World will not receive compensation from the park if they are injured whilst there.

Explanation = Based on the terms and conditions, we can see that Shark World accepts no responsibility for any harm that comes to visitors – therefore we can assume that they will not be paying out for compensation.

Q13. *Answer = C. Pay a fine.*

Explanation = The passage clearly states, 'Any person found staying in the park beyond their applicated time will be escorted from the premises by security, and asked to pay a fine.'

Q14. *Answer = C. The Council of North Ficshire*

Explanation = The passage is written by North Ficshire council, which shows that they are working with the owners of the park, to construct it.

Q15. *Answer = D. North Ficshire, one hundred, shark, risk.*

Q16. False

Q17. True

Q18. Impossible to Say

Q19. Impossible to Say

Q20. True

Q21. *Answer = C. Brian has written this guide as a manual for new employees, so they can learn the way that Marketing Gurus Inc functions on a day-to-day basis.*

Explanation = The central purpose of this manual is to show new employees how to behave in the workplace.

Q22. *Answer = A. Brian believes that Marketing Gurus Inc has a better understanding of what customers want, than the customer themselves.*

Explanation = The passage clearly states, 'Our customers want to buy our products, even if they don't know it. More than that, they *need* to buy our products. We know what's best for them.'

Q23. *Answer = C. Marketing Gurus Inc customers would rather be told about new products, than be told that they won't receive a refund*

Explanation = The paragraph states, 'What do you think a customer would prefer to hear, that there's no refund for £5000 they spent on our business enhancement programme, or that we've got a great new product they might be interested in? Your job is to make their day better.' Brian is asking a rhetorical question here – implying that the answer should be obvious.

Q24. *Answer = A. Brian believes that if a customer wants a refund, they simply haven't tried the product for long enough to be satisfied.*

Explanation = Brian clearly states, 'Here at Marketing Gurus Incorporated, we don't do refunds. A refund is just a customer acknowledging that they didn't try hard enough with the product. It's for their own good that we say no.'

Q25. *Answer = A. Customers pay £0.50 a minute to call Marketing Gurus Inc, therefore the more time they spend on the phone the more money the company makes.*

Explanation = Brian is essentially making a clever subversion on the phrase 'time is money' which usually infers that time costs money. In this case, time actually makes the company money – because they profit for every minute the customers spend on the phone.

Q26. *Answer = B. To entice customers to purchase more products, in the belief that they will become rich.*

Explanation = When we look at some of the buzzwords, 'entrepreneur', 'unlimited wealth', 'goldrush' and 'millionaire' these are clearly terms associated with wealth, written with the purpose of persuading people that they will become rich.

Q27. Paragraph 6

Q28. Paragraph 4

Q29. Paragraph 2

Q30. Paragraph 7

Q31. Paragraph 6

Q32. Paragraph 7

Q33. False

Q34. False

Q35. Impossible to Say

Q36. True

Q37. Impossible to Say

Q38. False

Q39. True

Q40. Impossible to Say

Speaking: About the Test

The IELTS speaking component is the same for both IELTS Academic and IELTS General Training. The speaking component is designed to assess your prowess in spoken English. It lasts for 11-14 minutes, and there are three parts to the test:

Part 1. In part 1, the examiner will ask you a series of general questions about yourself. This could include your hobbies, your family, where you work, what you study, what type of food you like to eat, and what pets you have. This part normally lasts around five minutes in total.

Part 2. In part 2, you will be given a card. The card will have a particular topic on it, and you will have one minute to prepare, before speaking for 2 minutes in total about the topic. Following this, the examiner will ask you a couple of questions about the subject.

Part 3. Part 3 involves the examiner asking further questions about the topic from part 2. The questions will be more complex, and you will have more of an opportunity to demonstrate your vocabulary, through the discussion of abstract ideas and issues related to the topic itself. This part of the assessment lasts for approximately 5 minutes in total.

How Is It Marked?

During the listening exercise, you will be scored on categories such as:

Fluency – which relates to your ability to link your ideas together and speak coherently, in clear English. The things you say must be logical, and the examiner will be looking at your use of spoken grammar, for example using conjunctions and connectors.

Vocabulary – your range of vocabulary will be assessed during this exercise. The words you use, the relevance and appropriateness of these words, and the ability to link words and ideas together using vocabulary is very important.

Pronunciation – your pronunciation is also being assessed. Your ability to pronounce words correctly is fundamental to passing this test. The assessor will be listening closely, to ensure that that speech is intelligent and precise, and that there is minimum strain from the speaker.

Obviously, we can't give a full practice session – as that would require us to be there asking you the questions. However, we've created a comprehensive set of questions which should test your ability to understand language, in a similar way that the assessors would test you. Have a go at these and see how you get on.

Before you begin, here's a guide on how to tackle our questions.

Speaking, Academic + General Training: Practice Questions

Each of the below tests will test you on something different, or require you to use different means to come up with the answer.

Below we've provided you with an example of how to answer each type of question that you'll encounter in these tests. You should refer back to these examples if you get stuck on how to do them.

**Please note, these are not the actual questions that you will face in the exam, they are simply to help you practise your language skills.*

PRACTICE TEST QUESTIONS AND ANSWERS

Each of the below tests will test you on something different, or require you to use different means to come up with the answer. Have a go at all of these tests, before comparing your answers with the ones at the back of the book.

Below we've provided you with an example of how to answer each type of question that you'll encounter in these tests. You should refer back to these examples if you get stuck on how to do them.

**Please note, these are not the actual questions that you will face in the exam, they are simply to help you practise your language skills.*

RESPONDING TO QUESTIONS

The first type of question that you'll see in our mock tests, requires you to pick the best response from a selection of answers.

For example, you might see a question such as this:

> *What was your favourite activity to do when you were a child?*

You'll then be given a selection of answers, like so:

A – When I was a child, I liked to play tennis with my father.

B – I played tennis.

C – Nowadays, I like to play squash with my friends.

D – Tennis.

All you need to do, is pick the best answer from the list. This one is fairly easy. Option C doesn't answer the question, and options B and

D are too short – so won't constitute a good response. Therefore, the answer is A.

COMPLETING THE MISSING LINE

The next type of question that you'll see in our mock tests, requires you to complete the missing line from a conversation. Again, you'll need to pick the best option from a selection of answers.

For example, you might see something like this:

> *Speaker A: Last week, I went to the doctors. It was quite a scary experience.*
>
> *Speaker B: Oh no, how come? Are you ill?*
>
> *Speaker A:*
>
> *Speaker B: Oh, what a relief, I'm really glad about that.*

As you can see, there is a gap where Speaker A should have responded. You will need to pick which answer option best fits in the gap. Pay close attention to how Speaker B has responded, because this should influence which answer option you pick:

A – Extremely. Unfortunately, the doctor has told me that I don't have long to live.

B – I was having severe headaches. Luckily the doctor diagnosed me as healthy.

C – After that, I played football with my friends.

D – I'm still having headaches.

The best answer option here is B. You can see that Speaker B has responded with 'what a relief, I'm really glad'. This is not something they would say if we'd picked answer option A or option D. Meanwhile, C doesn't answer the question.

INCORRECT WORDS

This type of question is fairly simple to complete.

You'll be given a conversation between two speakers, for example:

> *Speaker A: After this assessment, I'm going to meet my friend.*
>
> *Speaker B: Oh great, what are you going to do?*
>
> *Speaker A: We're probably going to go to the cinema, to see the new romance movie.*
>
> *Speaker B: That sounds like a lot of fun. I went to the headphones last week.*

If you look at this conversation, the last line doesn't make sense. The word 'headphones' shouldn't be there. Now look at the below answer options, and decide which word would be the best to replace it:

A – Betting

B – Cinema

C – Brown

D – Lorry

The best word in this instance would be 'Cinema'. So, the answer is B.

Another variation on this type of question, which you'll see during our mock tests, requires you to identify the word that is incorrect.

For example:

> *Matthew went to the park and bought a tinfoil from the food booth.*

A – Matthew

B – Tinfoil

C – Booth

D – Food

In this case, the answer would be 'tinfoil', as this is clearly incorrectly placed in the sentence.

COMPLETE THE NEXT LINE

For this type of question, you'll be given a sentence.

For example:

> *Next week, I am going to visit London with my friend. We will go out for dinner and then visit a bar.*

Your job is to complete the next sentence, using the answer options provided:

A – I was really excited for it.

B – I couldn't wait!

C – I'm really looking forward to it.

The answer here is C, as this is written in the future tense, which matches with the question.

REPLACE THE WORD

This type of question is very easy to complete. All you need to do, is replace the word written in capital letters, with the correct word from the answer options.

For example:

> *Last week, I went to visit my mother in hospital. Unfortunately, she is very BALLOON.*

A – Raisin

B – Lions

C – Sick

D – Orange

The best answer here is C, as none of the other words would make sense in this sentence.

REPLACE THE SENTENCE

In this type of question, you will be given a poorly worded sentence. You'll need to decide which answer option best replaces the sentence.

<u>For example:</u>

> *On Wednesday, I am going to buy a potty for my child. I was really excited to buy it, as it is an exciting time in my child's life.*

A – On Wednesday, I am going to buy a potty for my child. I am really excited to buy it, as it is an exciting time in my child's life.

B – On Wednesday, I am going to buy a potty for my child. I will be really excited to buy it, as it was an exciting time in my child's life.

The best answer option here is A, as it uses tenses correctly, unlike option B.

Now, have a go at the mock tests.

Speaking

TEST 1

QUESTION 1

What are your future career plans? Do you have any ambitions to move on from your current job?

A – I love my job, but I won't do it for the rest of my life.

B – I am a very ambitious person. I want to become a lawyer one day.

C – I love my job, but one day I hope to become a successful lawyer. I cannot stay at this company forever.

D – My job is great, but I am ambitious. I want to become a lawyer.

QUESTION 2

I believe that integrity is more important than winning. If you win without integrity, you may as well be SURFING.

A – Broken.

B – Losing.

C – Frowning.

D – Dead.

QUESTION 3

Speaker A: Are there any hobbies that you'd really like to try in the future?

Speaker B: I'd love to learn how to ice skate.

Speaker A: Ice skating, how interesting! Why do you want to learn that?

Speaker B:

A – Football players earn lots of money. I'd like to do the same.

B – Ice skating is a very graceful sport. It's a bit like dancing.

C – It looks fun.

D – Why do you want to learn how to play tennis?

QUESTION 4

What kind of music do you listen to?

A – I don't like music, it's boring. I'd rather play with the tools in my shed.

B – Yep, music is a great concept.

C – I listen to lots of 90s music. Especially songs that have appeared in films.

D – Somebody once told me that music is a waste of time.

QUESTION 5

How do you get to work in the mornings?

A – Train.

B – I take the train from Charing Cross Station to London Victoria, and from there I catch a bus to my office.

C – I get the train and then the bus.

D – I get a bus from the train station.

QUESTION 6

When you aren't working, what kind of things do you do in your free time?

A – I am always working.

B – I play video games.

C – I enjoy playing poker online. Last Sunday I made lots of money.

D – In my free time I like to sit in front of the TV.

QUESTION 7

Speaker A: It's really nice to meet you. What have you been up to this past weekend?

Speaker B: Doing bits buddy, and you?

Speaker A: Well I went to see my grandmother on Sunday, unfortunately she's terribly ill.

Speaker B: I'm delighted to hear that.

A – Weekend.

B – Unfortunately.

C – Terribly.

D – Sorry.

QUESTION 8

What do you think about the National Health Service (NHS)?

A – The NHS is a great service. In my country, you have to pay for medical care.

B – The NHS is very slow.

C – I admire the staff who work at the NHS.

D – One day, I would love to become a doctor, and this is what I'm currently training for.

QUESTION 9

My grandmother dies last week. In two days' time, I will attend her funeral.

A – I attended the funeral of my grandmother last week.

B – I am attend the funeral of my grandmother next week.

C – I would attend the funeral of my grandmother next week.

QUESTION 10

Gemma packs the boxes but she did it slow and is fired.

A – Gemma packed the boxes, but she did it slowly, and was fired.

B – Gemma packed the boxes, but she did it slow, and is fired.

QUESTION 11

Since you moved to England, have you tried any takeaway restaurants?

A – Yes.

B – Pizza.

C – I tried pizza. I didn't like it.

D – Yes, I tried pizza. Unfortunately, the place that we ordered from wasn't so good.

QUESTION 12

I went to the doctors, complaining about a FUNKY. He provided me with antibiotics.

A – Sand.

B – Beef.

C – Cough.

D – Henry.

QUESTION 13

> *I believe that the internet is a dangerous place for children. They should not be MUSTARD to go on there.*

A – When.

B – Allowed.

C – Seen.

D – Because.

QUESTION 14

> *Speaker A: Unfortunately, I'm not very good with money. My account manager keeps telling me to stop spending it on clothes.*
>
> *Speaker B: Ha ha, oh dear. I'm very good with money, luckily.*
>
> *Speaker A: What do you normally spend your money on?*
>
> *Speaker B:*
>
> *Speaker A: Ah, that's very kind of you.*

A – Usually I spend my money on essentials like food and drink, and then save the rest.

B – I spent a bit on food and drink, and then gamble the rest in the casino.

C – I give a lot of my money to charity.

D – I just don't spend it.

QUESTION 15

> *Are you married? Tell me about your partner.*

A – I have been married for 4 years now. My partner is named Michael, and he works in a printing shop.

B – Yes, I have been married for 4 years as of next week.

C – My partner is named Michael. He is rich.

D – Yes, we have been married for 4 years. Soon we will divorce.

TEST 2

QUESTION 1

> *Speaker A: That's great to hear that you completed your degree. What are your future career plans?*
>
> *Speaker B: Well, I'd like to write my own book.*
>
> *Speaker A: How exciting, do you have any ideas for what you'll write about?*
>
> *Speaker B: Not at the moment. How about you, what are your career plans?*
>
> *Speaker A:*

A – Well, after I leave here today I'm planning on going shopping with my mother.

B – Tonight I'll sit down and watch the news.

C – I already have a job.

D – I would love to be a professional interior designer. I like drawing and making things.

QUESTION 2

> *Yesterday, I went into the shops and bought a jacket and jeans. Unfortunately, the jacket was too PLASTIC for my liking, and the jeans were very ugly. I should have tried them on before I purchased them.*

A – Big.

B – Watery.

C – Fruity.

D – Cold.

QUESTION 3

> *Somebody once ask me to borrow money, as they have run out of change for gas.*

A – Somebody once ask me to borrow money, as they had run out of gas.

B – Somebody once asked me to borrow money, as they had run out of change for gas.

QUESTION 4

> *What do you think of the UK train system?*

A – It is bad.

B – Trains are always late in the UK.

C – I don't take the train.

D – UK train journeys are extremely expensive compared to elsewhere, and the service is bad.

QUESTION 5

> *Speaker A: It's great that you spend so much time with your friends.*
>
> *Speaker B: I know, I'm very lucky to have such good friends. How about you, do you see your friends a lot?*
>
> *Speaker A:*
>
> *Speaker B: That's a shame.*

A – No, most of them live back in my own country.

B – Yes, all the time. I live with 2 of them.

C – Friends are an expendable commodity.

D – Yes.

QUESTION 6

> *When I was a child, my father took me to the zoo. Unfortunately he was WEDDING by tigers.*

A – Drank.

B – Eaten.

C – Paid.

D – Raised.

QUESTION 7

> *What is the one thing that you miss more than anything, since moving to England?*

A – England is much better than my own country.

B – Although I love England, I miss my family, who stayed back at home.

C – The hot weather.

D – The food here is bland and uninteresting.

QUESTION 8

> *Ice skating was a dangerous sport. You could fell down and hurt yourself.*

A – Ice skating is a dangerous sport. You could fallen down and hurt yourself.

B – Ice skating is a dangerous sport. You could fall down and hurt yourself.

QUESTION 9

Speaker A: I've been in hospital for the past 2 weeks, with a serious medical condition.

Speaker B: Oh no, are you okay now though?

Speaker A: Yes, thank you. The NHS were extremely terrible, they took such good care of me.

Speaker B: I'm glad to hear it.

A – Medical.

B – Care.

C – Terrible.

D – Condition.

QUESTION 10

How do you find the weather in England?

A – Rainy!

B – It's very cold here compared to my own country.

C – Quite warm.

D – I find that people in England talk about the weather a lot.

QUESTION 11

> *Speaker A: I love going to the cinema. My favourite types of movies are comedies.*
>
> *Speaker B: Oh, I love the cinema too. I like comedies, but my favourite type of film is action.*
>
> *Speaker A: Did you see the new action film that is out? I heard that it's terrible.*
>
> *Speaker B: Yes, I went to see it last week. You are right, me and my friends thought it was fantastic.*
>
> *Speaker A: Yes, my friend went to see it and told me that he really didn't enjoy it.*

A – Fantastic.

B – Comedies.

C – Enjoy.

D – Cinema.

QUESTION 12

> *I do not feel comfortable dancing in nightclubs. There are too many people, and the music is extremely QUIET.*

A – Sad.

B – Tired.

C – Loud.

D – Dim.

QUESTION 13

> *My father make his money by sold clothing in the street markets.*

A – My father makes his money by selling clothing on the street market.

B – My father makes his money by sold clothing on the street market.

QUESTION 14

Tell me about your best friend.

A – His name is John.

B – My best friend is named John. He works at an insurance company.

C – John is my best friend.

D – My best friend is named John.

QUESTION 15

I hate the summer. It's too warm, and you can no longer wear a TOUPEE.

A – Coat.

B – Underwear.

C – Glasses.

D – Leotard.

- - - - - - - - - - - -
TEST 3
- - - - - - - - - - - -

QUESTION 1

I am terrified of little electric fans. They are extremely SALTY and could hurt you.

A – Fans.

B – White.

C – Dangerous.

D – Small.

QUESTION 2

Speaker A: My morning routine is pretty simple. I get up, brush my teeth, get dressed and then come downstairs for a bowl of cornflakes, before heading off to work.

Speaker B: And how do you get to work?

Speaker A: I get the train in, as the station is just five minutes from my house. How about you?

Speaker B:

Speaker A: Oh really? Perhaps one day we will be on the same train together.

A – I drive in to work, there are no trains in my area.

B – I catch the bus, it's very quick and easy.

C – I also get the train in, from Paddington Station.

D – I walk.

QUESTION 3

Do you have many friends? Why do you think it's important for people to have friends?

A – I have 4 or 5 close friends. They stop me from being lonely.

B – I don't have many friends. Friends make you weak.

C – I have 1 or 2 very close friends. Friends are important, they keep you motivated and energised.

D – I don't need friends.

QUESTION 4

Jacob had an accident in the office. Josh quickly grabbed the first-aid MONKEY.

A – Car.

B – Smell.

C – Kit.

D – Money.

QUESTION 5

Last weekend, I went to the cinema with my friend. The movie that we went to see was called Sarah and the Lighthouse.

A – Sarah and the Lighthouse was a great film, we really enjoyed it.

B – Sarah and the Lighthouse will be a great film, and we are looking forward to seeing it.

C – Sarah and the Lighthouse is a great film, and we are enjoying it.

QUESTION 6

Speaker A: Last weekend, I visited the zoo. I went with my family.

Speaker B: Oh, I love the zoo. How was your trip?

Speaker A:

Speaker B: That sounds fantastic!

A – It wasn't so good. I didn't like the animals very much.

B – It was great, thanks.

C – We had a really nice time. I loved seeing the giraffes.

D – Terrible. My father was eaten by the lions.

QUESTION 7

Do you ever watch the news?

A – No.

B – Sometimes, but not much.

C – The news is a government tool. It's a conspiracy.

D – I try to avoid it. I find the news very depressing.

QUESTION 8

Are you a fit and healthy person?

A – Yes

B – No, I smoke heavily and never exercise. I would say I'm slightly overweight.

C – Yes, but I only exercise occasionally.

D – Yes, I go jogging every day.

QUESTION 9

White bread are less healthier than brown bread, but it will taste so much better.

A – White bread is less healthy than brown bread, but it tastes so much better.

B – White bread is less healthier than brown bread, but it will taste so much better.

QUESTION 10

Do you watch much TV? Which is your favourite channel?

A – TV is a waste of time.

B – I love watching TV. My favourite channel is BBC1, as they have lots of nature programmes.

C – The BBC is my favourite channel.

D – My TV is broken.

QUESTION 11

Supermarket foods are deceptively bad for you. They contain lots of NEON ingredients and salt.

A – Red.

B – Soapy.

C – Extra.

D – Dead.

QUESTION 12

I try very hard. Unfortunately, it did not matters.

A – I tried very hard. Unfortunately, it did not matter.

B – I tried very hard. Unfortunately, it doesn't matters.

QUESTION 13

The town that I live in is quite unpleasant. The buildings are ugly, the roads are dirty, and the people are CAKE.

A – Old.

B – Rude.

C – Tall.

D – Late.

QUESTION 14

> *Speaker A: During weekdays, I work in an office, for a publishing company.*
>
> *Speaker B: That sounds interesting. What kind of tasks do you have to do?*
>
> *Speaker A: I help clients to put their books up on the internet, so that they can sell toast.*
>
> *Speaker B: Wow, that sounds a lot more interesting than my job. I'm just a factory worker.*

A – Factory.

B – Internet.

C – Tasks.

D – Toast.

QUESTION 15

> *On Wednesday, I will take the train into the town, and buy some Christmas presents for my mum.*

A – The presents I bought for my mum were very expensive.

B – Hopefully, I won't spend too much money on the presents.

C – The present is not very expensive.

TEST 4

QUESTION 1

> *I will not understand the appeal of video games. They have been a waste of our children's time.*

A – I do not understand the appeal of video games. They are a waste of our children's time.

B – I will not understand the appeal of video games. They are a waste of our children's time.

QUESTION 2

Do you have children? How would you describe your parenting style?

A – Yes, 3 children. I beat them regularly.

B – I have 3 children, but they don't live with me.

C – I have 3 children. I would describe my parenting style as firm but fair.

D – I have 3 children. They are badly behaved.

QUESTION 3

Have you ever been to a music festival?

A – Yes, we went to one last summer.

B – We went to a rock concert last summer. There were too many people. I hated it.

C – Music festivals are very loud, I don't like them.

D – Yes, once or twice.

QUESTION 4

Speaker A: My job involves a lot of prior planning and communication with other team members.

Speaker B: That sounds difficult, do you get paid very much?

Speaker A:

Speaker B: Wow, fantastic.

A – I get paid a bit higher than the average wage.

B – I can barely afford to buy bread for my family.

C – No.

D – I earn minimum wage.

QUESTION 5

My father has worked as a carpenter for many years now. He owns a CAVE in the town centre. He is very popular with the locals.

A – Shop.

B – Cave.

C – Centre.

D – Room.

QUESTION 6

The criminals torture Benjamin to see if they will broke him. Finally, Benjamin breaking.

A – The criminals tortured Benjamin to see if they could break him. Finally, Benjamin broke.

B – The criminals tortured Benjamin to see if they could broke him. Finally, Benjamin break.

QUESTION 7

Tell me about a day out that you had recently.

A – I went to Folkestone with my brother. We had a fantastic time.

B – I went to Folkestone last week. We went surfing and had a picnic.

C – I am always working.

D – Last Wednesday, I went to Folkestone for the day. We sat on the beach, ate a picnic and then went surfing in the sea. Both me and my brother had a fantastic time.

QUESTION 8

Speaker A: The school that I went to wasn't very good. We had lots of troublemaking students.

Speaker B: Oh, I didn't enjoy school either. I was bullied.

Speaker A:

Speaker B: Thanks. I'm glad school is over now.

A – That's really funny, I'm glad to hear it.

B – That's pretty silly of you.

C – That's sad, I'm sorry to hear that.

D – Why did you do that? I enjoyed History.

QUESTION 9

Speaker A: So, do you exercise much?

Speaker B: Sadly, no. I really should do more, especially since I'm a heavy smoker.

Speaker A: I used to smoke, but I gave up when I was aged calendar.

Speaker B: Yes, it's very hard to quit.

A – Calendar.

B – Smoke.

C – Exercise.

D – Heavy.

QUESTION 10

Last summer, I visited Croatia. Unfortunately, the weather was cold and PLASTERS.

A – Rainy.

B – Sunny.

C – Blue.

D – Emerald.

QUESTION 11

Speaker A: It's nice to meet you. How was your journey here? Did you have far to come?

Speaker B: It wasn't so bad. I only live 10 minutes away, so I walked.

Speaker A: Oh that's lucky. I live an hour away, so I got the helicopter.

Speaker B: Oh I used that last week, normally it's so full of people though.

A – Minutes.

B – Helicopter.

C – Journey.

D – Normally.

QUESTION 12

Speaker A: Do you play any sports?

Speaker B:

Speaker A: Oh me too! Along with that, I also play tennis, badminton and hockey.

Speaker B: That's great, which team do you support?

A – Yes, I play tennis and hockey occasionally.

B – Football, almost every single day. I play at the park with my friends.

C – I play lots of badminton. I'm on a team with my friends.

D – No, I'm not very sporty.

QUESTION 13

What made you decide to move to England?

A – The lifestyle in England is very good. There are plenty of opportunities for jobs and the government takes care of its citizens.

B – The weather.

C – England is a rich country with good opportunities.

D – I needed a job.

QUESTION 14

On Monday, I was going to the cinema. I saw the action film, with my friend and brother.

A – Next Monday, I am going to saw an action film. I'm going to the cinema with my friend and brother.

B – On Monday, I went to the cinema. I saw an action film, with my friend and my brother.

QUESTION 15

Last summer I go sailing with my brother. We capsized our boat and have to be rescued.

A – Last summer, I went sailing with my brother. We capsize our boat and must be rescued.

B – Last summer, I went sailing with my brother. We capsized our boat and had to be rescued.

TEST 5

QUESTION 1

> *What is your favourite food? Is there anything new that you've come to love since you arrived in England?*

A – English food is dull.

B – My favourite food is chicken and rice. Since I arrived in England, I have enjoyed a number of good pizza takeaways.

C – Rice is my favourite food.

D – I haven't enjoyed English food.

QUESTION 2

> *Speaker A: Do you spend much time browsing the internet?*
>
> *Speaker B: Oh yes, quite a lot actually. Especially when I first wake up in the morning.*
>
> *Speaker A: What sort of sites do you normally visit?*
>
> *Speaker B:*
>
> *Speaker A: Ah, I see. I generally try to avoid the news, as I find that it depresses me.*

A – Usually I visit gossip and showbiz websites. I love celebrity culture.

B – I mostly browse through news websites, to check up on world events.

C – The internet is a tool for the government to control us.

D – Music websites mostly, and video sites too.

QUESTION 3

I am not a fan of video games. I believe that they are to blame for violence, and that more people should spend JUMPER reading the Bible.

A – Money.

B – Liquor.

C – Time.

D – Smile.

QUESTION 4

Speaker A: How well do you get on with your family?

Speaker B: Sometimes good, sometimes bad. I argue a lot with my sister. Do you have any siblings?

Speaker A: No, I was an only child.

Speaker B: Do you still live with your family?

Speaker A:

A – Yes, I live with my sister and her boyfriend, and occasionally our brother visits us too.

B – We occasionally see our aunty, but that's about it. Both my grandparents died when I was young.

C – Yes, my mother and father own the house that we share together.

D – No.

QUESTION 5

Today, I am gone to the supermarket to bought groceries.

A – Today, I am going to the supermarket to buy groceries.

B – Today, I have going to the supermarket to buy groceries.

C – Today, I was going to the supermarket to buy groceries.

QUESTION 6

> *There is many conspiracies about the world. The most popular are the Illuminati.*

A – There is many conspiracies about the world. The most popular, is the Illuminati.

B – There are many conspiracies about the world. The most popular, is the Illuminati.

QUESTION 7

> *How often do you recycle? Are England's laws different to your own country?*

A – In my own country, we barely recycle. Here, the laws are much stricter, and I recycle every week.

B – I don't recycle. The environment is boring.

C – Global warming is a conspiracy.

D – The laws here are different. I recycle more than I did at home.

QUESTION 8

> *Speaker A: My children just became eligible to join an English primary school.*
>
> *Speaker B: That's great, my children have been going to English schools for some time now.*
>
> *Speaker A: How do you find English schools compared to the schools back in your own country?*
>
> *Speaker B:*
>
> *Speaker A: Ah yes, I have heard that they are very organised and less strict. That makes me feel less nervous.*

A – From my experience, English schools are very organised. However there are less rules than schools in my own country.

B – From my experience, English schools are quite disorganised. They are less strict than in my own country though.

C – I hate English schools.

D – English schools subjected my child to bullying and torment. Home-school your child, before it's too late.

QUESTION 9

Which do you prefer, going out for the day or staying in?

A – I like to go out and meet people.

B – I prefer staying in. It is warmer.

C – Going out for the day. I love to explore, especially big cities.

D – Staying in is better.

QUESTION 10

How well do you get on with your family?

A – Not very. We are always fighting.

B – I get on well with them.

C – My family don't live in England, so I rarely see them.

D – Quite well. I am very close to my aunty and to my mother. I don't see much of my father though, as he is in prison.

QUESTION 11

When I bought a new laptop, the first thing I always do is installed anti-virus software.

A – When I bought a new laptop, the first thing I always do is install anti-virus software.

B – When I buy a new laptop, the first thing I always do is install anti-virus software.

QUESTION 12

Last week we cleaned out our water filter. It was disgusting and filled with CUSTARD.

A – Mould.

B – Lions.

C – Pens.

D – Sherbet.

QUESTION 13

When you were at school, what subjects did you take? Which was your favourite?

A – History, Maths and English.

B – I took a lot of different subjects at school, including: Maths, History and English.

C – I took Maths, History and English at school. My favourite, however, was Geography.

D – School is boring.

QUESTION 14

The house I'm bought was the middle of nowhere. It was at a hill, on top of trees and flowers.

A – The house that I bought was in the middle of nowhere. It was on top of a hill, with trees and flowers below.

B – The house that I'm buying was on top of a hill. There were trees and flowers below it.

QUESTION 15

How often do you go shopping? What is your favourite shop?

A – I don't like shopping. Last weekend I bought a jacket that was too big and some bootcut jeans.

B – I loved shopping. My favourite place to shop is Yves Saint Laurent, although the prices are a little high.

C – Shopping is for girls.

D – Sometimes I go to the supermarket and buy pens.

TEST 6

QUESTION 1

Red is my favourite colour. I like red because it is the same colour as BROWN.

A – Apples.

B – Bananas.

C – Money.

D – Bread.

QUESTION 2

Every day, we ordered from the sandwich shops. It make us very fat.

A – Every day, we ordered from the sandwich shop. It made us very fat.

B – Every day, we ordered from the sandwich shop. It makes us very fat.

QUESTION 3

> *Speaker A: I think one of the biggest differences between England and my own country, is how much recycling is done here.*
>
> *Speaker B: Yes, in my country, recycling isn't a major priority.*
>
> *Speaker A: How much do you recycle?*
>
> *Speaker B:*
>
> *Speaker A: Ah yes, me too. I find that filling one bin a week with recyclable material is quite hard though, and I'm always putting stuff in the wrong bin.*

A – As per our council requirements, one recycling bin a week is taken away by the rubbish collectors.

B – As per our council requirements, we must fill up at least 3 bins with recyclable material per week.

C – If we do not recycle, we will be sent to prison.

D – I don't recycle.

QUESTION 4

> *Excuse me, how much does this item cost? I would like to purchase it please.*

A – That item was fourteen pounds and ninety-nine pence.

B – That item is fourteen pounds and ninety-nine pence.

C – That item can be fourteen pounds and ninety-nine pence.

QUESTION 5

> *Speaker A: Where do you normally shop?*
>
> *Speaker B: For clothes? Or food? For food, I usually go to my local supermarket.*
>
> *Speaker A: How about for clothes?*
>
> *Speaker B:*

A – I prefer shopping online for my clothes, it makes the whole process much easier.

B – Like I said, I go to my local supermarket for food.

C – I don't go clothes shopping.

D – I hate clothes.

QUESTION 6

People who steal music from the internet are doing irreparable damage to the industry. These people should be treated as MILK.

A – Milk.

B – Refugees.

C – Royalty.

D – Criminals.

QUESTION 7

At twenty past eight this morning, I got the WASPS into work.

A – Bus.

B – Sandwich.

C – Calculator.

D – Bath.

QUESTION 8

Last year, I got into lots of trouble. I failed to declare lots of my income, and the taxman JUMPED me.

A – Ate.

B – Penalised.

C – Kicked.

D – Beat.

QUESTION 9

> *Speaker A: I went to university in Brighton.*
>
> *Speaker B: Oh, Brighton is really nice. What did you study there?*
>
> *Speaker A: Philosophy and Media. How about you, did you go to university?*
>
> *Speaker B:*

A – I went to school in London, but I didn't enjoy it very much.

B – No, I didn't go to university. I started working right after I left school.

C – One day in the future, perhaps I would go to university.

D – When I visited Brighton, we spent the day on the beach.

QUESTION 10

> *Martin Luther King Day was celebrate on the third January Monday of every year.*

A – Martin Luther King Day is celebrated on the third Monday of January, every year.

B – Martin Luther King Day was celebrated on the third Monday, every year, in January.

QUESTION 11

> *Unfortunately, I am colour-blind. This means that I cannot see certain colours, such as red and DESK.*

A – Clue.

B – Singe.

C – Blue.

D – Sue.

QUESTION 12

Speaker A: I'm still looking for a job, I've found it surprisingly difficult.

Speaker B: Oh, me too. I have a job but it took me ages to get one.

Speaker A: What job did you do before you moved to England?

Speaker B: I worked for a building supply company. We sold cement, bricks and bread to our customers.

A – Building.

B – Surprisingly.

C – Bread.

D – Ages.

QUESTION 13

Speaker A: Well, I first moved to England about 5 years ago. How about you?

Speaker B: I've only been here for 2 years.

Speaker A: How do you find it? Is it very different to your home country?

Speaker B:

A – The weather is very different, and the food is quite bland. However, I like living here.

B – It's very cold.

C – No, I prefer my own country.

D – Your home country is much nicer than mine.

QUESTION 14

Samuel Smith goes to the shops. He has buy three pens, a ruler and a gravy boat.

A – Samuel Smith is going to the shops. He bought three pens, a ruler and a gravy boat.

B – Samuel Smith went to the shops. He bought three pens, a ruler and a gravy boat.

QUESTION 15

Speaker A: Since moving to England, what's been your least favourite thing?

Speaker B: I love England…but probably the weather. It's just so cold and rainy.

Speaker A: Yes, the English weather isn't so good. In my country it's quite cold too though, so I'm used to it.

Speaker B:

Speaker A: Ah, I can see how you have found it difficult to adjust then.

A – Yes, in my country it's very cold too.

B – In my country, it almost never rains, and is very hot.

C – My country has lots of snow and ice.

D – My country has similar weather to England.

TEST 7

QUESTION 1

Speaker A: I don't eat meat, because I'm a vegetarian.

Speaker B: Oh, that's very noble of you. I wish I had the willpower to be a vegetarian.

Speaker A: Yes, it is hard sometimes, especially when meat smells so tissue.

Speaker B: Maybe I will give it a try.

A – Tissue.

B – Noble.

C – Willpower.

D – Vegetarian.

QUESTION 2

> *Last week, I went to a festival. The music was very loud, and there were lots of drunk SALMON walking round.*

A – Cowboys.

B – Elephants.

C – People.

D – Cats.

QUESTION 3

> *I have an eating disorder. The disorder means that I am eating objects such as pen, paper and plastics.*

A – I have an eating disorder. The disorder means that I eat objects such as pens, paper and plastic.

B – I have a eating disorder. The disorder means that I eaten objects such as pens, paper and plastic.

QUESTION 4

> *Sue's husband had decided to divorce her. She threw his clothes out of the window. He was very YELLOW.*

A – Fluffy.

B – Angry.

C – Pain.

D – Roast.

QUESTION 5

Tell me about your hometown. What is it like?

A – I grew up in Lisbon. The weather is much hotter than England, but the economy is poor. Lisbon is a big city, a bit like London, with lots of things to keep you entertained.

B – I grew up in Lisbon. The weather is better, but that's all.

C – Don't be so nosy.

D – I grew up in Lisbon. While the weather is better in Portugal, there are much more things to do here in England.

QUESTION 6

Speaker A: I hated school, but I still think that education is really important.

Speaker B: I agree. Why do you think it is so important?

Speaker A: Education teaches us important life skills. A lack of education can make people ignorant.

Speaker B: Yes, that's right. I never had a good education really.

Speaker A: That's a shame.

Speaker B: It's okay, it's dogs.

A – Education.

B – Ignorant.

C – Dogs.

D – Important.

QUESTION 7

I go to the dentist and she tell me that I eat too many sweet. My teeth are rotting.

A – I went to the dentist, and she told me that I eat too many sweet.

My teeth are rotten.

B – I went to the dentist, and she told me that I eat too many sweets.
My teeth are rotten.

QUESTION 8

Speaker A: Tell me about something that you loved doing as a child.

Speaker B: Well, when I young, I loved to play tennis with my father. We'd go down to the local tennis court and play for 2 hours, every Sunday. Sadly, my father is now in prison.

Speaker A: That's a shame, do you mind if I ask why?

Speaker B: He was embezzling funds for his football school. I no longer speak to him. Anyway, what did you love doing as a child?

Speaker A:

Speaker B: Oh that's awesome, I love hockey. It's great that you reached such a high level.

A – When I was young, I played lots of hockey. I played for a team for several years.

B – In my younger days, I loved football. I reached quite a high level.

C – I played lots of hockey. I was so good that I had trials for my country.

D – I played hockey, but wasn't particularly good at it.

QUESTION 9

Speaker A: I read in the newspaper recently that the Queen is thinking of visiting Manchester.

Speaker B: Really? I would love to meet the Queen.

Speaker A: Me too, she's such an inspiring person.

Speaker B: If she visits Manchester, maybe I will see if I can swimming her.

A – Inspiring.

B – Manchester.

C – Swimming.

D – Newspaper.

QUESTION 10

Susan arrived late to work today. Her boss pointed his finger and said, 'You're MELTING.'

A – Scary.

B – Distant.

C – Fired.

D – Ugly.

QUESTION 11

I do not watch UK soaps. They are unrealistic and filled with REDWIND actors.

A – Poorly.

B – Poor.

C – Wealthy.

D – Sarcastic.

QUESTION 12

> *Speaker A: It's coming up to Christmas now, are you excited?*
>
> *Speaker B: Oh yes, very. We do celebrate Christmas in my country, but it's not quite such a big deal.*
>
> *Speaker A: Yes, in the UK Christmas is a huge occasion. I couldn't believe all of the decorations around town. Have you bought any gifts for anyone this year?*
>
> *Speaker B:*
>
> *Speaker A: Oh how lovely, I'm sure she'll appreciate that. I wish I had enough money to buy my sister a car too, but she'll just have some socks instead.*

A – Yes, I spent very big this year. I have bought my sister a holiday.

B – Yes, but I haven't spent much. I bought my sister some shampoo.

C – Yes, I spent quite a lot this year. I have bought my sister a new car.

D – Bah, humbug.

QUESTION 13

> *Speaker A: Last summer we went to Spain, did you take any trips recently?*
>
> *Speaker B: I prefer to stay at home, to be honest. How was your trip to Spain?*
>
> *Speaker A:*
>
> *Speaker B: That's a shame. I hear that Barcelona is much nicer, so maybe you should go there next time instead.*

A – Not good, unfortunately. We stayed in Barcelona, but the weather was horrid.

B – Dreadful. We stayed in Madrid, but the city is so ugly, and I don't like the football team either.

C – Great, thanks. We stayed in Bilbao. It was really sunny and relaxing.

D – We had a fantastic time. We stayed in Mallorca, which is a really lovely place.

QUESTION 14

Pete goes to fetch the ball from his neighbour's house. He can be never seen again.

A – Pete went to fetch the ball from his neighbour's house. He was never seen again.

B – Pete went to fetch the ball from his neighbour's house. He is never seen again.

QUESTION 15

Tell me about your mother. What job does she do?

A – My father works at the local supermarket.

B – My mother is named Claire.

C – My mother is named Claire. She works at the local supermarket, and is 46 years old.

D – Don't speak about my mother.

Speaking: Answers

TEST 1

Q1.

What are your future career plans? Do you have any ambitions to move on from your current job?

Answer = C – I love my job, but one day I hope to become a successful lawyer. I cannot stay at this company forever.

Q2.

I believe that integrity is more important than winning. If you win without integrity, you may as well be SURFING.

Answer = B – Losing.

Q3.

Speaker B:

Answer = B – Ice skating is a very graceful sport. It's a bit like dancing.

Q4.

What kind of music do you listen to?

Answer = C – I listen to lots of 90s music. Especially songs that have appeared in films.

Q5.

How do you get to work in the mornings?

Answer = B – I take the train from Charing Cross Station to London Victoria, and from there I catch a bus to my office.

Q6.

When you aren't working, what kind of things do you do in your free time?

Answer = C – I enjoy playing poker online. Last Sunday I made lots of money.

Q7.

Speaker B: I'm **delighted** to hear that.

Answer = D – Sorry.

Q8.

What do you think about the National Health Service (NHS)?

Answer = A – The NHS is a great service. In my country, you have to pay for medical care.

Q9.

My grandmother dies last week. In two days' time, I will attend her funeral.

Answer = A – I attended the funeral of my grandmother last week.

Q10.

Gemma packs the boxes but she did it slow and is fired.

Answer = A – Gemma packed the boxes, but she did it slowly, and was fired.

Q11.

Since you moved to England, have you tried any takeaway restaurants?

Answer = D – Yes, I tried pizza. Unfortunately, the place that we ordered from wasn't so good.

Q12.

I went to the doctors, complaining about a FUNKY. He provided me with antibiotics.

Answer = C – Cough.

Q13.

I believe that the internet is a dangerous place for children. They should not be MUSTARD to go on there.

Answer = B – Allowed.

Q14.

Speaker B:

Answer = C – I give a lot of my money to charity.

Q15.

Are you married? Tell me about your partner.

Answer = A – I have been married for 4 years now. My partner is named Michael, and he works in a printing shop.

TEST 2

Q1.

Speaker A:

Answer = D – I would love to be a professional interior designer. I like drawing and making things.

Q2.

Yesterday, I went into the shops and bought a jacket and jeans. Unfortunately the jacket was too PLASTIC for my liking, and the jeans were very ugly. I should have tried them on before I purchased them.

Answer = A – Big

Q3.

Somebody once ask me to borrow money, as they have run out of change for gas.

Answer = B – Somebody once asked me to borrow money, as they had run out of change for gas.

Q4.

What do you think of the UK train system?

Answer = D – UK train journeys are extremely expensive compared to elsewhere, and the service is bad.

Q5.

Speaker A:

Answer = A – No, most of them live back in my own country.

Q6.

When I was a child, my father took me to the zoo. Unfortunately he was WEDDING by tigers.

Answer = B – Eaten.

Q7.

What is the one thing that you miss more than anything, since moving to England?

Answer = B – Although I love England, I miss my family, who stayed back at home.

Q8.

Ice skating was a dangerous sport. You could fell down and hurt yourself.

Answer = B – Ice skating is a dangerous sport. You could fall down and hurt yourself.

Q9.

Speaker A: Yes, thank you. The NHS were extremely **terrible**, they took such good care of me.

Answer = C – Terrible.

Q10.

How do you find the weather in England?

Answer = B – It's very cold here compared to my own country.

Q11.

Speaker B: Yes, I went to see it last week. You are right, me and my friends thought it was **fantastic**.

Answer = A – Fantastic.

Q12.

I do not feel comfortable dancing in nightclubs. There are too many people, and the music is extremely QUIET.

Answer = C – Loud.

Q13.

My father make his money by sold clothing in the street markets.

Answer = A – *My father makes his money by selling clothing on the street market.*

Q14.

Tell me about your best friend.

Answer = B – *My best friend is named John. He works at an insurance company.*

Q15.

I hate the summer. It's too warm, and you can no longer wear a TOUPEE.

Answer = A – *Coat.*

TEST 3

Q1.

I am terrified of little electric fans. They are extremely SALTY and could hurt you.

Answer = C – *Dangerous.*

Q2.

Speaker B:

Answer = C – *I also get the train in, from Paddington Station.*

Q3.

Do you have many friends? Why do you think it's important for people to have friends?

Answer = C – I have 1 or 2 very close friends. Friends are important, they keep you motivated and energised.

Q4.

Jacob had an accident in the office. Josh quickly grabbed the first-aid MONKEY.

Answer = C – Kit.

Q5.

Last weekend, I went to the cinema with my friend. The movie that we went to see was called Sarah and the Lighthouse.

Answer = A – Sarah and the Lighthouse was a great film, we really enjoyed it.

Q6.

Speaker A:

Answer = C – We had a really nice time. I loved seeing the giraffes.

Q7.

Do you ever watch the news?

Answer = D – I try to avoid it. I find the news very depressing.

Q8.

Are you a fit and healthy person?

Answer = B – No, I smoke heavily and never exercise. I would say I'm slightly overweight.

Q9.

White bread are less healthier than brown bread, but it will taste so much better.

Answer = A *– White bread is less healthy than brown bread, but it tastes so much better.*

Q10.

Do you watch much TV? Which is your favourite channel?

Answer = B *– I love watching TV. My favourite channel is BBC1, as they have lots of nature programmes.*

Q11.

Supermarket foods are deceptively bad for you. They contain lots of NEON ingredients and salt.

Answer = C *– Extra.*

Q12.

I try very hard. Unfortunately, it did not matters.

Answer = A *– I tried very hard. Unfortunately, it did not matter.*

Q13.

The town that I live in is quite unpleasant. The buildings are ugly, the roads are dirty, and the people are CAKE.

Answer = B *– Rude.*

Q14.

Speaker A: I help clients to put their books up on the internet, so that they can sell **toast**.

Answer = D – Toast.

Q15.

On Wednesday, I will take the train into the town, and buy some Christmas presents for my mum.

Answer = B – Hopefully, I won't spend too much money on the presents.

TEST 4

Q1.

I will not understand the appeal of video games. They have been a waste of our children's time.

Answer = A – I do not understand the appeal of video games. They are a waste of our children's time.

Q2.

Do you have children? How would you describe your parenting style?

Answer = C – I have 3 children. I would describe my parenting style as firm but fair.

Q3.

Have you ever been to a music festival?

Answer = B – We went to a rock concert last summer. There were too many people. I hated it.

Q4.

Speaker A:

***Answer = A** – I get paid a bit higher than the average wage.*

Q5.

My father has worked as a carpenter for many years now. He owns a CAVE in the town centre. He is very popular with the locals.

***Answer = A** – Shop.*

Q6.

The criminals torture Benjamin to see if they will broke him. Finally, Benjamin breaking.

***Answer = A** – The criminals tortured Benjamin to see if they could break him. Finally, Benjamin broke.*

Q7.

Tell me about a day out that you had recently.

***Answer = D** – Last Wednesday, I went to Folkestone for the day. We sat on the beach, ate a picnic and then went surfing in the sea. Both me and my brother had a fantastic time.*

Q8.

Speaker A:

***Answer = C** – That's sad, I'm sorry to hear that.*

Q9.

Speaker A: I used to smoke, but I gave up when I was aged **calendar**.

Answer = A – Calendar

Q10.

Last summer, I visited Croatia. Unfortunately, the weather was cold and PLASTERS.

Answer = A – Rainy.

Q11.

Speaker A: Oh that's lucky. I live an hour away, so I got the **helicopter**.

Answer = B – Helicopter.

Q12.

Speaker B:

Answer = B – Football, almost every single day. I play at the park with my friends.

Q13.

What made you decide to move to England?

Answer = A – The lifestyle in England is very good. There are plenty of opportunities for jobs and the government takes care of its citizens.

Q14.

On Monday, I was going to the cinema. I saw the action film, with my friend and brother.

Answer = B – On Monday, I went to the cinema. I saw an action film, with my friend and my brother.

Q15.

Last summer I go sailing with my brother. We capsized our boat and have to be rescued.

Answer = B – Last summer, I went sailing with my brother. We capsized our boat and had to be rescued.

TEST 5

Q1.

What is your favourite food? Is there anything new that you've come to love since you arrived in England?

Answer = B – My favourite food is chicken and rice. Since I arrived in England, I have enjoyed a number of good pizza takeaways.

Q2.

Speaker B:

Answer = B – I mostly browse through news websites, to check up on world events.

Q3.

I am not a fan of video games. I believe that they are to blame for violence, and that more people should spend JUMPER reading the Bible.

Answer = C – Time

Q4.

Speaker A:

Answer = C – Yes, my mother and father own the house that we share together.

Q5.

Today, I am gone to the supermarket to bought groceries.

***Answer = A** – Today, I am going to the supermarket to buy groceries.*

Q6.

There is many conspiracies about the world. The most popular are the Illuminati.

***Answer = B** – There are many conspiracies about the world. The most popular, is the Illuminati.*

Q7.

How often do you recycle? Are England's laws different to your own country?

***Answer = A** – In my own country, we barely recycle. Here, the laws are much stricter, and I recycle every week.*

Q8.

Speaker B:

***Answer = A** – From my experience, English schools are very organised. However there are less rules than schools in my own country.*

Q9.

Which do you prefer, going out for the day or staying in?

***Answer = C** – Going out for the day. I love to explore, especially big cities.*

Q10.

How well do you get on with your family?

Answer = D – Quite well. I am very close to my aunty and to my mother. I don't see much of my father though, as he is in prison.

Q11.

When I bought a new laptop, the first thing I always do is installed anti-virus software.

Answer = B – When I buy a new laptop, the first thing I always do is install anti-virus software.

Q12.

Last week we cleaned out our water filter. It was disgusting and filled with CUSTARD.

Answer = A – Mould.

Q13.

When you were at school, what subjects did you take? Which was your favourite?

Answer = C – I took Maths, History and English at school. My favourite, however, was Geography.

Q14.

The house I'm buying was the middle of nowhere. It was at a hill, on top of trees and flowers.

Answer = A – The house that I bought was in the middle of nowhere. It was on top of a hill, with trees and flowers below.

Q15.

How often do you go shopping? What is your favourite shop?

Answer = A – I don't like shopping. Last weekend I bought a jacket that was too big and some bootcut jeans.

TEST 6

Q1.

Red is my favourite colour. I like red because it is the same colour as BROWN.

Answer = A – Apples.

Q2.

Every day, we ordered from the sandwich shops. It make us very fat.

Answer = A – Every day, we ordered from the sandwich shop. It made us very fat.

Q3.

Speaker B:

Answer = A – As per our council requirements, one recycling bin a week is taken away by the rubbish collectors.

Q4.

Excuse me, how much does this item cost? I would like to purchase it please.

Answer = B – That item is fourteen pounds and ninety-nine pence.

Q5.

Speaker B:

Answer = A – I prefer shopping online for my clothes, it makes the whole process much easier.

Q6.

People who steal music from the internet are doing irreparable damage to the industry. These people should be treated as MILK.

Answer = D *– Criminals.*

Q7.

At twenty past eight this morning, I got the WASPS into work.

Answer = A *– Bus.*

Q8.

Last year, I got into lots of trouble. I failed to declare lots of my income, and the taxman JUMPED me.

Answer = B *– Penalised.*

Q9.

Speaker B:

Answer = B *– No, I didn't go to university. I started working right after I left school.*

Q10.

Martin Luther King day was celebrate on the third January Monday of every year.

Answer = A *– Martin Luther King Day is celebrated on the third Monday of January, every year.*

Q11.

Unfortunately, I am colour-blind. This means that I cannot see certain colours, such as red and DESK.

Answer = C – Blue.

Q12.

Speaker B: I worked for a building supply company. We sold cement, bricks and bread to our customers.

Answer = C – Bread.

Q13.

Speaker B:

Answer = A – The weather is very different, and the food is quite bland. However, I like living here.

Q14.

Samuel Smith goes to the shops. He has buy three pens, a ruler and a gravy boat.

Answer = B – Samuel Smith went to the shops. He bought three pens, a ruler and a gravy boat.

Q15.

Speaker B:

Answer = B – In my country, it almost never rains, and is very hot.

TEST 7

Q1.

Speaker A: Yes, it is hard sometimes, especially when meat smells so tissue.

Answer = A – Tissue.

Q2.

Last week, I went to a festival. The music was very loud, and there were lots of drunk SALMON walking round.

*Answer = **C** – People.*

Q3.

I have an eating disorder. The disorder means that I am eating objects such as pen, paper and plastics.

*Answer = **A** – I have an eating disorder. The disorder means that I eat objects such as pens, paper and plastic.*

Q4.

Sue's husband had decided to divorce her. She threw his clothes out of the window. He was very YELLOW.

*Answer = **B** – Angry.*

Q5.

Tell me about your hometown. What is it like?

*Answer = **A** – I grew up in Lisbon. The weather is much hotter than England, but the economy is poor. Lisbon is a big city, a bit like London, with lots of things to keep you entertained.*

Q6.

Speaker B: It's okay, it's dogs.

*Answer = **C** – Dogs.*

Q7.

I go to the dentist and she tell me that I eat too many sweet. My teeth are rotting.

Answer = B – I went to the dentist, and she told me that I eat too many sweets. My teeth are rotten.

Q8.

Speaker A:

Answer = C – I played lots of hockey. I was so good that I had trials for my country.

Q9.

Speaker B: If she visits Manchester, maybe I will see if I can swimming her.

Answer = C – Swimming.

Q10.

Susan arrived late to work today. Her boss pointed his finger and said, 'You're MELTING.'

Answer = C – Fired.

Q11.

I do not watch UK soaps. They are unrealistic and filled with REDWIND actors.

Answer = B – Poor.

Q12.

Speaker B:

Answer = C – Yes, I spent quite a lot this year. I have bought my sister a new car.

Q13.

Speaker A:

Answer = B *– Dreadful. We stayed in Madrid, but the city is so ugly, and I don't like the football team either.*

Q14.

Pete goes to fetch the ball from his neighbour's house. He can be never seen again.

Answer = A *– Pete went to fetch the ball from his neighbour's house. He was never seen again.*

Q15.

Tell me about your mother. What job does she do?

Answer = C *– My mother is named Claire. She works at the local supermarket, and is 46 years old.*

Listening: About the Test

The IELTS Listening assessment is the same for both IELTS Academic and IELTS General Training. It is designed to assess your ability to understand spoken English. There are four sections to the listening assessment, consisting of 10 questions each. The test-taker will listen to each section, then answer 10 questions based on that section. The test lasts for 30 minutes, with 10 minutes to answer each section. After each recording, you will have 10 minutes to answer, before moving onto the next recording.

We have recorded four different tests, which you can sample via the following link:

www.IELTSListening.co.uk

Once you've listened to each speech recording, go through the related questions in the next section, before moving onto the next one.

The sections are as follows:

Recording 1. The first recording will be of two people, and will be set in an everyday setting. For example, you might hear two people discussing the weather, or an upcoming party.

Recording 2. The second recording will be a monologue, again set in an everyday environment/subject. For example, you might hear somebody discussing what they do for their job.

Recording 3. The third recording will be of up to four people, and will be set in an educational or work-based/training environment. For example, you might hear students discussing their essay topic, or employees talking with their boss.

Recording 4. The final recording will be of a monologue, set in an educational environment. So, you might somebody discussing an academic subject.

The main thing that the assessors are looking for in this test, is your ability to understand ideas and information, plus opinions and viewpoints of speakers. Your ability to take in information and understand this, through what you have heard, is fundamental to this exercise.

There are a variety of question types that you might face in this exam:

Task 1

Task 1 consists of multiple-choice type questions. You'll have to choose between three possible answers to a question, or you'll be asked to complete a sentence, again choosing between three possible answers.

For example, you might be asked:

What did Lydia say she would arrive at Ben's birthday party?

A – Seven o'clock.

B – Nine o'clock.

C – Five o'clock.

Task 2

In task 2, candidates are required to match a list of numbered items from the text, with a set of options. For example, if one of the speakers is trying to book a hotel, but they need the hotel to match certain criteria. You'll be given a list of criteria, and then asked to decide which one best fits with requirements of the speaker. For example:

Look at the below lists and decide which one would be suitable for Mark, given his requirements:

Name: Hotel Alaban

Location: Spain

Facilities: Swimming Pool, Restaurant, Gift Shop

Child friendly: No

Name: Hotel California

Location: London

Facilities: Golf course, Gym

Child friendly: Yes

Task 3

In task 3 candidates are asked to complete labels on a diagram, based on what they've heard on the recording. For example, you might be asked to name the places on a map, based on what the speakers have said, or fill in their individual locations. The aim of this task is to ensure that the candidate understands verbal descriptions, and can mentally relay this in the form of visual recreation, or following instructions.

Task 4

In task 4, candidates will be asked to fill in gaps in a diagram or written information, using what they've heard in the text. You will be given a word limit for each gap, or you may be given a set of answers from which to choose.

Task 5

In task 5, candidates are asked to complete a series of sentences, containing missing words. The candidate then has to fill in the missing word, using information from the text. Again, you will be given a word limit for this, which will be specified in the question.

For example:

Complete the missing word in the below sentence. Use TWO WORDs only.

Martin's argument with ….   ……… heated, and the boss had to step in.

Answer = Ben, became.

Task 6

In task 6, candidates are asked to read a question based on the text, and then write a short answer using what they've heard. Again, you will be given a word limit.

For example:

Why did Ben decide to punch Martin? Answer in 5 words or less.

Answer = He was angry about Jane.

Now, have a go at our sample questions!

You can download the recordings via **www.IELTSListening.co.uk**

Listening, Academic + General Training: Practice Questions

Recording 1

Answer the following questions based on what you heard:

Q1. Which of the following is true?

A – Lilith and Bryan work for a company called LendzNLetz.

B – Bryan is the boss of the company.

C – Walter will fire Bryan the next day.

Q2. Complete the following sentence, based on what you've heard:

After Bryan told her that he was pretending to be ill, Lilith decided…

A – not to tell anyone about what he'd said.

B – to try and convince her boss to fire Bryan.

C – to pretend to be ill herself.

Q3. Which of the following statements is incorrect?

A – Lilith was unwell, and therefore took the day off work.

B – Walter considered firing Bryan, after this incident.

C – Walter's surname is Smith.

Take a look at the sentences below and then assign each sentence to a particular speaker, based on what you heard. Some of the sentences have been paraphrased.

Q4.

'I was out picking up some medicine.'

'Kevin deserved to lose his job.'

'Walter is a harsh manager.'

Q5.

'LendzNLetz should come before any individual employee.'

'I'm feeling terrible.'

'I'll consider firing Bryan.'

Q6. Based on what you've heard, which of the following diagrams most accurately summarises the positions of people within the company.

A	B	C
BRIAN	LILLITH	WALTER
LILLITH — WALTER	BRIAN — WALTER	LILLITH — BRIAN

Q7. Which of the following is implied by what you've heard:

A – Lilith has tried to persuade Bryan to fire Walter in the past.

B – Bryan has asked Walter for a meeting, to discuss his employment status.

C – Lilith has tried to persuade Walter to fire other employees in the past.

D – Walter is exceptionally difficult to please.

Q8. Complete the following, based on what you've heard:

…… and ….. bumped into each other. Both of them ………. that they were ….. to be ….. Following that, ….. rang …….. at his office, telling …. that ………. should consider …….. ………. .

A – Steve, Bryan, realised, faking, ill. Steve, Lilith, her, she, hiring, Lilith.

B – Walter, Steve, reminisced, eligible, hired, Steve, Bryan, Lilith, Walter, firing, Steve.

C – Lilith, Bryan, admitted, pretending, ill, Lilith, Walter, him, he, firing, Bryan.

D – Angelo, Mary, forgot, meant, working, Steve, Angelo, her, Bryan, a, paycut.

Q9. Which of the following statements is true?

A – Lilith told Bryan that she was pretending to be ill, who told Walter, who told Steve.

B – Bryan told Walter that Steve told him he was pretending to be ill. Steve then told Lilith.

C – Bryan told Lilith that he was pretending to be ill, who told Walter.

Q10. Which of the following best summarises what Lilith said to Walter?

A – Lilith believed that Bryan should lose his job, because lying had a negative impact on the company.

B – Lilith believed that Bryan should lose his job, because he had been stealing from the company.

C – Lilith believed that Bryan should lose his job, because he had undermined her.

D – Lilith believed that Bryan should lose his job, because he had disrespected Walter.

Recording 2

Answer the following questions based on what you heard:

Q11. Which of the following does Jakob believe to be true?

A – That Ficshire Rail treats its customers with the utmost respect.

B – That Ficshire Rail's delays cannot be justified.

C – That Ficshire Rail's fees are extortionate.

Q12. Which of the following does Jakob use to justify the criticisms regarding delays?

A – There aren't enough delays, for long enough, to justify the criticism.

B – People in general are very ungrateful.

C – People have paid a low amount for the service, so they should expect a service representative of that.

Q13. Which of the following best summarises Jakob's role in the company?

A – Jakob works as an electrical engineer. His job is to make sure that the trains are clean, tidy, and presentable.

B – Jakob works as a sound engineer. His job is to make sure the radio announcements are running smoothly.

C – Jakob works as a construction engineer. His job is to make sure that trains are running smoothly and on time.

Q14. Which of the following is implied by the speech?

A – Jakob's boss forced him to speak positively about the company, when he really didn't want to.

B – Jakob decided to make a positive speech about the company, out of gratitude for the career they've given him.

C – Jakob hates his job, and is looking for work elsewhere.

Q15. What does Jakob use to explain his lack of care over the rail fares?

A – Jakob believes that the rail fares represent good value for money.

B – Jakob gets free lunches, and a good pension.

C – Jakob gets to ride the trains for free.

Q16. Which of the following is NOT implied by the speech?

A – Jakob's skills and expertise will ultimately lead to a better paying, more satisfying, career.

B – Ficshire Rail have been criticised by the newspapers.

C – Jakob's boss wants to enhance the reputation of Ficshire Rail.

Complete the following table, sorting the sentences into true or false, based on the speech. If a sentence is not mentioned in the speech, you should sort this into false.

Q17. Ficshire Rail treats its employees well.

Q18. Ficshire Rail cares about its customers.

Q19. People have high standards.

Q20. Jakob often deals with train power failure.

TRUE	FALSE

Recording 3

In the below questions, your task is to look at each statement, and then assign it to a speaker, based on what you heard.

Q21. 'Trotsky was inferior to Stalin.'

Q22. 'Stalin was a boring man, with a distasteful sense of humour.'

Q23. 'Britain won the war.'

Q24. 'Martin is immature.'

Q25. 'Assignments must be in by the end of the week.'

Now, answer the following questions based on what you heard:

Q26. Which of the following is true?

A – Martin has missed his deadline, and will lose marks as a result.

B – Mr Gibbons is worried that Steve has deviated from the main subject of the essay.

C – Alicia thinks that Martin is stupid and immature.

Q27. Which of the following people is described as 'the worst of Stalin's cronies'?

A – Beria

B – Molotov

C – Steve

Q28. What does Martin use to justify his dislike of Stalin?

A – He doesn't appreciate Stalin's sense of humour.

B – He thinks Churchill was better.

C – He believes Stalin lucked out, and didn't really defeat Hitler.

Q29. Which of the following best summarises Alicia's view of Stalin?

A – She thought he was extremely attractive when he was younger.

B – She was mesmerised by videos of his political speeches.

C – She thinks that Trotsky would have been a better candidate for leadership.

Q30. Which of the following best summarises Mr Gibbons's view of the assignment?

A – Mr Gibbons would prefer to receive a piece of work explaining why Stalin was superior to Trotsky.

B – Mr Gibbons would prefer to receive a piece of work explaining why Trotsky was superior to Stalin.

C – Mr Gibbons doesn't care whether the students prefer Stalin or Trotsky, he just wants it handed in on time.

Recording 4

Answer the following questions based on what you heard:

Q31. Which of the following is the correct title, for Andrew Smugley-Bunton's position?

A – Lead Coordinator for the Ficshire Creative Writing programme.

B – Lead Instructor for the Ficshire Junior Writing programme.

C – Lead Marker for the Ficshire Non-Fiction Writing programme.

Q32. Which of the following is implied by Andrew Smugley-Bunton?

A – You could lose marks if you fail to attend his congratulatory gatherings.

B – You will gain marks if you produce writing that is similar in style to the course lecturers.

C – Students on the course are expected to behave in a way befitting a Master's candidate.

Q33. Which of the following best summarises the central aim of Initiation?

A – To show students how superior Andrew Smugley-Bunton's work is, compared to theirs.

B – To help students develop their own style and quality of writing.

C – To introduce students to the course and their fellow candidates.

Sort the statements below into the table, according to which part of the course they fall under.

Q34. 'One-to-one sessions with a tutor'

'Teaching a creative writing seminar'

'Submitting a portfolio of evidence'

Q35. 'Seminar focused discussion'

'A 15,000-word piece of writing'

'Getting feedback from lecturers and students'

Q36. 'An 8000-word piece of writing'

'Three tasks, over 6 weeks'

'Providing evidence that their writing has improved*

INITIATION	INTERMEDIARY	CONCLUSION

Fill in the missing sentences below, with the relevant word from the speech.

Q37. The central aim of the after-class gatherings, is so that Andrew Smugley-Bunton can hear how ……… he is, from his fellow …… .

A – amazing, students.

B – fantastic, writers.

C – terrible, lecturers.

D – woeful, scholars.

Q38. The after-class gatherings will be held at ………

A – Anderson Grove

B – Anderson Chapel

C – Anderton Tower

D – Anderton Hall

Q39. In their second term, students will be asked to submit a portfolio of evidence, to show that…

A – They have completed all of the challenges set by the lecturers.

B – They have read the complete collection of books, by Andrew Smugley-Bunton.

C – They are willing to accept that they will never be as talented, as Andrew Smugley-Bunton.

D – They have improved the quality of their writing.

Q40. During the 'Conclusion' element of the course, students must submit a piece of work consisting of ..... words.

A – 7000

B – 2000

C – 8000

D – 15,000

Listening: Answers

Q1. *Answer = A. Lilith and Bryan work for a company called LendzNLetz.*

Explanation = Based on the conversation they have, it is heavily implied that Lilith and Bryan work for LendzNLetz.

Q2. *Answer = B. to try and convince her boss to fire Bryan.*

Explanation = Based on the speech, it is clear that Lilith made the decision to try and persuade her boss, Walter, to fire Bryan.

Q3. *Answer = A. Lilith was unwell, and therefore took the day off work.*

Explanation = This statement is incorrect, because Lilith admits to lying about being ill.

Q4.

'I was out picking up some medicine.'

Answer = Lilith

'Kevin deserved to lose his job.'

Answer = Lilith

'Walter is a harsh manager.'

Answer = Bryan

Q5.

'LendzNLetz should come before any individual employee.'

Answer = Lilith

'I'm feeling terrible.'

Answer = Lilith

'I'll consider firing Bryan.'

Answer = Walter

Q6.

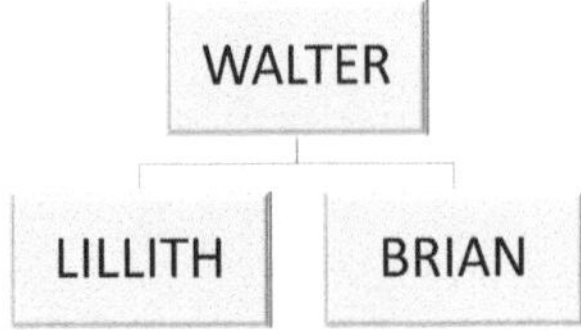

Q7. *Answer = C. Lilith has tried to persuade Walter to fire other employees in the past.*

Explanation = Lilith states, 'Maybe you should fire him, we can't have liars in the company. I told you this before, with Steve, but you didn't listen to me.'

Q8. *Answer = C. Lilith, Bryan, admitted, pretending, ill, Lilith, Walter, him, he, firing, Bryan.*

Explanation = **Lilith** and **Bryan** bumped into each other. Both of them **admitted** that they were **pretending** to be **ill**. Following that, **Lilith** rang **Walter** at his office, telling **him** that **he** should consider **firing Bryan**.

Q9. *Answer = C. Bryan told Lilith that he was pretending to be ill, who told Walter.*

Explanation = This is the only answer which makes sense in context of the passage.

Q10. *Answer = A. Lilith believed that Bryan should lose his job, because lying had a negative impact on the company.*

Explanation = Lilith states, 'Maybe you should fire him, we can't have liars in the company.'

Q11. *Answer = C. That Ficshire Rail's fees are extortionate.*

Explanation = Jakob clearly states, 'Whilst I fully understand about the extortionate fees, as a day's return to London costs more than an entire day's wages for me…'

Q12. *Answer = A. There aren't enough delays, for long enough, to justify the criticism.*

Explanation = Jakob states, 'It's only five minutes here and there, every other hour. If that's not good enough then I just don't know what to tell you…'

Q13. *Answer = C. Jakob works as a construction engineer. His job is to make sure that trains are running smoothly and on time.*

Explanation = Jakob states, 'I work in the construction department, as an engineer. My role is to ensure that Ficshire Rail trains are running smoothly and on time, every single day.'

Q14. *Answer = A. Jakob's boss forced him to speak positively about the company, when he really didn't want to.*

Explanation = Near the end of the monologue, Jakob states, 'My boss, Kenneth…even told me that if I didn't speak highly of the railway today, I'd lose my job.'

Q15. *Answer = C. Jakob gets to ride the trains for free.*

Explanation = In relation to the rail fares, Jakob states, 'I actually get to ride the trains for free…so I don't really care.'

Q16. *Answer = A. Jakob's skills and expertise will ultimately lead to a better paying, more satisfying, career.*

Explanation = Answer A is not implied, in any way, shape or form, by the monologue.

Q17, 18, 19, 20.

TRUE	**FALSE**
Ficshire Rail treats its employees well.	Ficshire Rail cares about its customers.
People have high standards.	
Jakob often deals with train power failure.	

Q21. *'Trotsky was inferior to Stalin.'*

Answer = Alicia

Q22. *'Stalin was a boring man, with a distasteful sense of humour.'*

Answer = Martin

Q23. *'Britain won the war.'*

Answer = Martin

Q24. *'Martin is immature'*

Answer = Steve

Q25. 'Assignments must be in by the end of the week.'

Answer = Mr Gibbons

Q26. Answer = B. Mr Gibbons is worried that Steve has deviated from the main subject of the essay.

Explanation = When responding to Steve, Mr Gibbons states, 'Although I'm worried you might have gone off topic a bit…'

Q27. Answer = A. Beria

Explanation = Mr Gibbons refers to Beria as 'probably the worst of Stalin's cronies.'

Q28. Answer = A. He doesn't appreciate Stalin's sense of humour.

Explanation = Martin states, 'I don't like Stalin, and I don't like the way he went about securing power, or his sense of humour.'

Q29. Answer = A. She thought he was extremely attractive when he was younger.

Explanation = Alicia clearly states, 'I got distracted by looking at photos of Stalin from when he was younger…whew what a looker.' This implies that she thought he was very attractive.

Q30. Answer = C. Mr Gibbons doesn't care whether the students prefer Stalin or Trotsky, he just wants it handed in on time.

Explanation = Mr Gibbons states, 'Whichever approach you take is fine, just as long as it gets done.'

Q31. Answer = A – Lead Coordinator for the Ficshire Creative Writing programme.

Explanation = Andrew Smugley Bunton describes himself as, 'the lead coordinator of the Ficshire University Creative Writing Masters programme.'

Q32. Answer = A. You could lose marks if you fail to attend his congratulatory gatherings.

Explanation = Andrew Smugley Bunton states, 'Please note that failing to attend these events, or to congratulate me, could have an impact on your final mark for the course.'

Q33. *Answer = B. To help students develop their own style and quality of writing.*

Explanation = The monologue states, 'During the first part, students will take part in seminars focused on improving their writing style and quality.'

Q34, 35, 36.

INITIATION	INTERMEDIARY	CONCLUSION
'Seminar focused dicussion'	'Submitting a portfo-lio of evidence'	'A 15,000-word piece of writing'
'Getting feedback from lecturers and students'	'Teaching a creative writing seminar'	'One-to-one sessions with a tutor'
	'Three tasks, over 6 weeks'	
	'Providing evidence that their writing has improved'	
	'An 8000 word piece of writing'	

Q37. *Answer = B. fantastic, writers*

Explanation = The central aim of the after-class gatherings, is so that Andrew Smugley Bunton can hear how **fantastic** he is, from his fellow **writers**.

NOTE: Pay attention to the word 'fellow'. This means that the second answer cannot be anything other than 'writers'

Q38. *Answer = D. Anderton Hall*

Explanation = The monologue states, 'Throughout the year, there will be a number of gatherings – after seminars, down at Anderton Hall.'

Q39. *Answer = D. They have improved the quality of their writing.*

Explanation = The monologue states, 'Secondly, students will be asked to put forward a portfolio of evidence, showing the ways in which their writing has progressed during that term.'

Q40. Answer = D. 15,000.

Explanation = The monologue states, 'At the end of the third part of the programme, students will be asked to submit a final piece of writing, consisting of 15,000 words.'

You have now reached the end of your guide to the IELTS examination, and no doubt you feel more prepared to tackle the assessments. We hope you have found this guide an invaluable insight into the test, and understand the expectations regarding your assessment.

For any type of test, we believe there are a few things to remember in order to better your chances and increase your overall performance.

REMEMBER – THE THREE Ps!

1. Preparation. This may seem relatively obvious, but you will be surprised by how many people fail their assessment because they lacked preparation and knowledge regarding their test. You want to do your utmost to guarantee the best possible chance of succeeding. Be sure to conduct as much preparation prior to your assessment to ensure you are fully aware and 100% prepared to complete the test successfully. Not only will practising guarantee to better your chances of successfully passing, but it will also make you feel at ease by providing you with knowledge and know-how to pass your IELTS examinations.

2. Perseverance. You are far more likely to succeed at something if you continuously set out to achieve it. Everybody comes across times whereby they are setback or find obstacles in the way of their goals. The important thing to remember when this happens, is to use those setbacks and obstacles as a way of progressing. It is what you do with your past experiences that helps to determine your success in the future. If you fail at something, consider 'why' you have failed. This will allow you to improve and enhance your performance for next time.

3. Performance. Your performance will determine whether or not you are likely to succeed. Attributes that are often associated with performance are self-belief, motivation and commitment. Self-belief is important for anything you do in life. It allows you to recognise your own abilities and skills and believe that you can do well. Believing that you can do well is half the battle! Being fully motivated and committed is often difficult for some people, but we can assure you that, nothing is gained without hard work and determination. If you want to succeed, you will need to put in that extra time and hard work!

Good luck with your IELTS test. We wish you the best of luck with all your future endeavours!

The how2become team

The How2Become Team

CHECK OUT OUR OTHER IELTS GUIDE:

FOR MORE INFORMATION ON OUR REVISION GUIDES, PLEASE CHECK OUT THE FOLLOWING:

WWW.HOW2BECOME.COM

WANT TO LEARN EVEN MORE REVISION TRICKS?

CHECK OUT OUR OTHER GUIDES:

FOR MORE INFORMATION CHECK OUT THE FOLLOWING:

WWW.HOW2BECOME.COM

Get Access To

FREE

Psychometric Tests

www.PsychometricTestsOnline.co.uk

Printed and bound by CPI Group (UK) Ltd, Croydon, CR0 4YY

08/06/2026

02131509-0002